Remembering
THE DON

A rare record of earlier times
within the Don River Valley
Charles Sauriol

Consolidated Amethyst Communications Inc.

Canadian Cataloguing in Publication Data
Sauriol, Charles, 1904
REMEMBERING THE DON
Text in English
I. Elphick, John II. Title
All Rights Reserved
© COPYRIGHT 1981
by Consolidated Amethyst Communications Inc.

ISBN 0-920474-22-5

Consolidated Amethyst Communications Inc.
60 Barbados Boulevard, Unit 6,
Scarborough, Ontario M1J 1K9

1st Printing — November 1981

Contents

Dedication

This book is dedicated to those descendants of Don Valley pioneer families, and other persons who in my time lived along or in the valley. To those scoutmasters, and boys of the East Toronto 45th troop of Boy Scouts who, in 1920, introduced me to the forks of the Don and beyond, and from this many unforgettable and happy camping experiences as a boy.

To my hiking companions, photographers, botonists, and nature lovers, and cross country skiers. To members of the Don Valley Conservation Association, with whom I fought many a battle to save the valley. To my associates in conservation, and particularly those of the Metropolitan Toronto and Region Conservation Authority. To that dynasty of Don Valley beekeepers of whom today there remains not a trace. In a later day, to those more recent companions of the Outing Club of East York, who instituted the Charles Sauriol annual tree planting day, and who have identified a nature sanctuary in the Don Valley with my name. All the foregoing contributed in some measure, directly or indirectly to the writing of "The Cardinal".

Finally to my parents, my wife and four children, in recollection of the friendly cottage, the orchard, the garden and from these values in country living the memories of the unforgettable, happy summers we passed in the valley, when the forks of the Don (then in a sylvan state) seemed a far cry from the Toronto of that time, and the wooded reaches of the valley and its meandering Don as remote as Algonquin Park.

Introductory Photographs

This scene from the brush of Fred Finlay O.S.A. depicts the manner in which men of the North-West company pulled their heavy bateaux up the steep cliffs of Hogg's Hollow. They rowed up the Don, to the forks of the stream, then up the west branch of the river to a landing place on a line with Yonge Street where it crosses the hollow today. The Yonge Street passage was a short cut to the Great Lakes; an alternative route to the Ottawa River, or the circuitous journey by Lake Erie.

Salmon fishing at night. This print from 'Picturesque Canada', shows a scene commonplace at one time on the Don and other Southern Ontario streams flowing into Lake Ontario. Plate courtesy Ontario Department of Planning and Development.

This print is reproduced from 'Canadian Illustrated News' of June 10th, 1871. In this same issue appears this text: 'There is one spot in the vicinity of Muddy York which all visitors to the Queen City of the west should make a point of visiting. The valley of the Don, a winding stream that flows on the east of the city, offers the prettiest bit of landscape in the neighbourhood, and is deserving of far more attention from lovers of the picturesque than it usually attracts. The sketch we reproduce is a faithful representation of the scene in the valley of the meander of Eastern Ontario.' Editor's note: the sketch was made at a point which would today correspond with Don Mills Road by the bridge over the forks of the Don, looking northwest.

Ice Jam on the Don by the bridge at King and Queen Street. Sketch from *Canadian Illustrated News*, March 9, 1878.

'Castle Frank' stood on the plateau of the steep and lofty slope on the west side of the Don Valley a few hundred yards south of the present Prince Edward viaduct. On January 23rd, 1796, Mrs. Simcoe wrote: 'The house is called Castle Frank built on the plan of a Grecian Temple totally of wood. The large pine trees make pillars for the porticos, which are at each end 16 feet high.' The Simcoes made use of the building as a summer residence from the Spring of 1794, until July 19th, 1796. In 1829 'Castle Frank' was burnt to the ground. In 1813, American troops ransacked it in their search for the papers and gold of the British garrison of York. Plate, courtesy Dept. Planning and Development.

Photo taken in 1948. Note west Don extreme left, east Don extreme right, Don Mills Road in centre. Refreshment booth is now replaced by Don Valley School of Art Chalet. De Grassi homestead situated behind willows in background. Exit from the valley here known as De Grassi Hill. Semi-detached houses on left built in 1907 for hired men of Thorncliff farm.

In the interest of historical accuracy all captions to photographs read as originally published in The Cardinal.

Introduction

It is all of thirty years since having completed a history of the Don Valley, I took my manuscript to a publisher. The good man kept it for a few weeks, then returned it to me with a curt note: "No one would be interested in what I had written. There would be no sale for this kind of book." So my consistent work and effort of the fifteen years or so that it took to write the story, struck the pavement of oblivion, or so it seemed.

I was convinced, however, that some of the stories I had written should appear in print, and devised a way to arrive at this end. In 1949, The Don Valley Conservation Association was a thriving, powerful (in its way) organization. It needed a medium of its own, to record its activities and from this, *The Cardinal* came into being. As a publication it would also include these choice segments of history of the Don Valley that I had so laboriously accumulated over the years.

The Cardinal was launched in the spring of 1951 as a modest eight-page pamphlet. By the end of that year it took on its permanent form; glossy paper, half-tones and line drawings for illustrations, typeset and no advertising content.

During the years that it appeared, it fell to me to write every word of it, to plan it, and to get it into production — a rather laborious task, all other commitments considered, until the last issue appeared, as planned, under date of March 15th, 1956.

The Cardinal's paper stock was a gift, the printing cost a bargain, and each in turn, the engraving firms of Toronto accepted to make the electrotypes, zinc etchings, and half-tones as their contribution to the aims and objectives of the Don Valley Conservation Association. The total run was one thousand copies. A Don Valley Conservation Association member received his copy free. The remaining copies remained with me. At the termination of publishing *The Cardinal* sequence, these copies were assembled into sets, several of which found their way into libraries, or reached the hands of persons who required a full set for a particular purpose.

For twenty-five years the hibernated *Cardinal* ceased virtually to breath. Occasionally I referred to it, or someone would call about it, that was all. The plates were destroyed by workmen when I lost my cottage up the Don, but the basic photos, and drawings remained secure in my files.

Quietly I began to hear more and more about *The Cardinal*, as it became a source of research for University students who were interested in both the Don Valley people of my time, and the history of the Don Valley. Some of these students came to my home and talked for hours about these subjects. I began to conclude that in *The Cardinal*, something had been achieved of a permanent nature.

One of the reserve sets was given to Barry Penhale. In 1968 I had been associated with Barry for a short while by assisting him with his publication 'The Outdoorsman'. We met frequently in the DeGrassi cottage at the Forks of the Don, which proved to be a comfortable place to work, and through these contacts, he got to know of *The Cardinal*.

In the summer of 1980, Barry, who had become a book publisher, suggested to me that extracts from *The Cardinal* should be published in book form. He showed me a selection of his preferences for this purpose. I was incredulous. Who in the general public would want to read anything I had written. Time had dulled my sensibilities of *The Cardinal's* worth beyond the student use, as noted.

Barry persisted and we agreed to proceed with this book, the text being very much as it was written by me so long ago.

I now look back on the past thirty years somewhat as a man who from a humble platform, has been catapulted into space — meaning that I have since had a meteoric career in conservation. The Don Valley Conservation Association was engulfed in the course of events, including the unforeseen development pressures that took place along the valleys and the amalgamation of The Don Valley Conservation Authority into The Metropolitan Toronto and Region Conservation Authority.

Out of the crucible of what seemed lost battles, I emerged in 1957 as Chairman of the Conservation Areas Advisory Board, M.T.R.C.A. and member of the Executive Committee, a role which I filled for fourteen years. In the sequence of events I lost all of my Don Valley property, and I lived with the nightmare of the construction of the Don Valley Parkway, and its companion in concrete, the trunk sewer. But also, despite the losses, I lived with my memories, and in the joy of being in good health to still use what had been saved.

The valleys became the locale for new uses and new people. The D.V.C.A. having been laid gently to its rest, was followed by organizations including Pollution Probe, which replaced in concept our pantomime of Governor Simcoe's trip to Richmond Hill, with the burial of the Don River through a funeral service held in view of the Bloor Street viaduct; an incongruity that did not survive in the face of planning for the lower Don Valley.

My dream of a wilderness at Toronto's doorstep was not practical, although some of it came true. Whereas I had so often gone to bed at night full of the bitterness of some defeat, I lived to enjoy new aspects of a Valley system I helped to preserve.

To these experiences of today, are added the memories of a half century— those of a boy who enjoyed the discovery of a new world of camping in a then wilderness—memories of the spring by the railway tracks, of the thimble berries that we picked near the ruins of Sam and Art Martin's cabin alongside McLean's sugar shanty. To one who first saw woods at fourteen, this was paradise!

Then memories of a young man's concern for his own future and associating with it, the consolation of miles of trails. These akin to the truest friend, always provided solace and consolation. Seeking en route the old ruins, and the old people to enquire what this ruin might have been, and how that plant got there.

When I acquired, in 1927, an old rundown cottage at the forks of the Don, a new life opened for me. Then I had four acres of my own. They filled my diary of those years with the stories and doings of a country place exactly two miles from where I lived.

This part of my experience may be unique. Each month of May my family moved two miles from city to country in as complete a transition as though the places were 200 miles apart.

My summers were passed there, summers that filled my time with the orchard, the garden, the apiary, the easy living by the then clean Don River, where the sound of water tumbling over the stones could be heard from my bedroom.

My valley experiences included an all-day walk from the west valley to the east valley, through native woods and farm fields, crowded today with plazas, shopping centres, traffic arteries and people. They were walks heightened in summer by an hour in a raspberry patch or a late afternoon dip in Clay Banks swimming hole.

It was a sad day indeed when I stood in the livingroom of my cottage at the Forks of the Don, and saw for the first time an expanse of blue sky above, from which song birds could be heard while workmen, wielding crowbars and axes, tore my world apart around me. That was my contribution to the Don Valley Parkway. Stoically I moved across the river, stored in the woodshed the pieces of my orchard trees that had been cut with chain saws, moved the bees' hives and for ten years, business was resumed as usual.

A second bolt of lightening struck in the same place, or more precisely, across the Don on the old DeGrassi place. For ten years I plied my trade here, to paraphrase Thoreau, as a collector of what the seasons offered, plus the management of a thriving apiary of 18 hives. Early in January 1968 I was mentally stunned to be told abruptly that I would have to get out. For a second time my world fell apart.

In the hasty retreat that followed, I took up a new country life on 20 acres north of Tweed. It was a holding pattern which compensated me in its way, although I never severed my roots from the valleys and in some respects, like the groundhogs, sunk them deeper in their soil. There is ample reason for this love of hearth and home, for the latter faces west looking into

Rosedale and the setting sun of any day of the 365—and I need merely jump the fence to enjoy walks that take me past old time haunts.

Parts of the valleys have gone to grass-mowed areas and picnic tables, and to people whose pursuits are revealed in the odour of cooking hamburgers, or in the panting breath of joggers, or in the hum of bicycle tires, or the family groups of trail skiers. There are still stretches of the valleys as I love them—the jungles of sweet clover, the stands of catnip, the old lilac bushes, the swimming hole, the springs, the campfire sites where the new groves of trees cover slopes once denuded by cattle or perennial grass fires or groves of pine trees that have scarcely changed in generations. From a point of vantage I sit on, to sometimes hear the hum of the interminable traffic of the Don Valley Parkway, and to which I am still paying toll (and reflect on my long friendship with the Valley).

Many writings of my own came from those years: Fourteen years on four acres; History of the Don Valley—the Don Valley as I knew it; Diary of a Conservationist; Ashes and Embers; The Seasons; One Man's Harvest. With the exception of *The Cardinal*, they have remained celebrities in solitude, arranged on my book shelves, constrained to a single copy each; also there were the diaries (shelves of them) to enable me to recall the harvest of my years.

During the past fourteen years, I have seen many valleys. Necessarily so, for as Projects Director of The Nature Conservancy, they are to be searched out and saved as nature reserves valleys from the east coast to the west coast. Escarpment land, wetlands, ecological reserves.

What I do here is part of my work. The Don Valleys from the circumstances of my association with them, went deeper, they were a part of me, as was *The Cardinal* which portrayed part of the life I had lived.

Having now been brought down from the shelves, I trust that it will again reach out to people whose interest in those far off days will be to me a source of deep appreciation.

THE **CARDINAL**

NO. 15   TORONTO, SEPTEMBER 15, 1954   25 Cents per copy

Selected Extracts
The Cardinal 1951-1956

Fall 1951

Wild Honey!

A LONG TIME AGO, in January of 1904, a group of men stood watching the upper Don River in premature flood. It was a balmy day of sixty degrees temperature, months ahead of its time. One of the men, tired of watching the heaving ice floes, struck a hollow basswood tree with a stick. As he did so, a number of bees appeared from a crevice high up the trunk. He again stuck the tree, and more bees appeared. The men were interested. Some discussion took place. Here was a bee tree; often read about but seldon seen and always intriguing as to contents.

An hour later three men returned to the tree. They carried a cross-cut saw, an axe, and several pails. In a few minutes the tree was down. It was a shell; four inches of rim, the rest hollow. As the tree fell, it broke near the top, exactly on a line with the bees' quarters. Out they came by the thousands, bewildered and angry. One of the men, this tale from the old 'Toronto World' relates, improvised a mask. He moved along to the entrance of the rustic hive, cleared away the debris, found the cache of succulent honey and filled a pail with the finest of the product of the nectar. He filled a second and a third pail. To quote the 'Toronto World':
'It is many a day since over a hundred pounds of honey have been taken from a bee tree in the third week in January, when the temperature was above sixty degrees and the river was running a great flood on the flats. Ten days before, forty pounds of honey had been taken from a tree a mile below the spot.'

And in conclusion W.F.McLean, M.P. for East York who penned the quoted lines, adds: 'Two bee trees loaded with honey seven miles from the city hall of Toronto with its 300,000 population ... only the beautiful valley of the Don could furnish it.'

The Don Valley bees of 1904 and those of today can usually store up honey in a manner satisfying to the beekeeper. The slightest warmth will bring the bees 'out-of-doors', so we find them in the early spring filling their saddle bags with pollen, from willow catkins, and elm bloom. They can also be seen on the congealed sap which gathers along the crevices of maple trees where winter storms have broken the branches. Then follow the first wild flowers, and the dandelions. By early summer if conditions are favourable the avalanche of honey begins to roll in millions of journeys to the hives. The bees will seek out clover, alfalfa, corn tassels, buckwheat, bugloss, willow herb, fire weed, wild roses, milkweed, wild sunflowers, cone flowers, blue vervain, the flowers of the basswood (bee) tree, catnip, and

24

many many others. It has been said that over 1,800 plants, shrubs, trees, yield nectar; some yield pollen only, which is also a food which the bee needs.

It is assumed that the nectar is an inducement to the bee to carry pollen from flower to flower; fertilizing many plants otherwise unfruitful. Certain flowers which at times overflow with nectar, will, under different weather conditions, remain dry. Almost every plant has its own peculiarities. The most common plants may in one season yield their nectar freely, yet in other seasons, for reasons best known to Mother Nature, they may produce but a scant supply of nectar.

Even with 'suburbia' closing in on the approaches to long reaches of the valley where wild flowers and wild crops once grew in abundance, it can still be said that the Don Valley is the paradise of the honey bee. That spoonful of fragrant honey which comes from the valley and which you smear on your buttered toast, may in its essence contain as much romance as aroma. It may have come from nodding trilliums, or from shy hepatica bloom, whose petals were blinking in the strong light of an April sunshine when the bee came across them, or months later from the ragged purple robes of the New England aster, or from the golden wand of the goldenrod.

The honey bee knows all the plants on which to draw for food and many a weary mile it travels along the reaches of the Don Valley; as lonely as an Indian Scout. Filling saddle bags again and again with the precious life-giving pollen, and gorging itself with equally precious nectar which it will later turn into honey. It is said that one tablespoon of honey which you and I take so much as a matter of course is the measure of a single bee's life-time work.

Fall 1951

What is a Green Belt?

SATURDAY MORNING: LATE JUNE. A small man could be seen trudging along Don Mills Road by the steep hill flanking Todmorden Park. He rounded the bend in the road, skirted Tumpers Mount, came to a concrete arch bridge, paused there then moved along an old farm road, crossed a creek on the delapidated remains of a bridge, picked up the thread of the road somewhat strangled by burdock plants, walked along it, then discovered a well-beaten trail extending along the middle of the valley wall and through an elm wood. High-arched elms shaded the graceful slope. Raspberry bushes closed in tightly along the trail, full with the promise of a crop to come. He came to another slope, walked up some steps which someone had cut in the sod, followed another trail to a bluff. An expanse of valley land met his gaze— the stream, the Don, wound its course through the centre of it. He climbed down a trail cut in this slope as well, made his way to the river shore, sat under a hawthorn. A catbird seemed anxious about his presence. Anyone would know that it was a catbird, but not so easy to guess was the soft whistling note from across the meadow.

The water pattering over the river stones fascinated him, as it would a little child. He removed his shoes, stockings, bathed his feet. Everything was luxuriantly green. His ears still hummed with the sound of the giant mixers alongside of which he worked every day. A distant rumble, every few seconds, told of motor cars striking the loose planking of the highway bridge; cars, rolling swiflty along Don Mills Road, fleeing the city towards the lake, as though the former was in the grip of a pestilence. But there was no such escape for him—a small salary, a small flat, and three small children. There would be no lake for them. That was his lot. He had been born on a farm, but his children had never seen much more of the outdoors than the trees on the street on which he lived. That was why he had come here. He had heard of this place, this valley. The papers described it as part of a Green Belt, whatever that was. His thoughts were tied more closely to factory belts. Green Belt was an empty word to him—a scheme probably to tap the money of people who could afford to build houses right on the edge of valleys such as this; surrounded with woods, where they could live their own little lives; shut off from the likes of him on the other side of the big traffic artery.

But come to think of it, no one had ordered him off the property. People he had met had been kind to him. He could ramble through here all he wanted providing he did not destroy anything.

The next day, Sunday, he returned—with his wife and children. They brought a lunch basket. This time he came to the stream by an easier route, to a little park they called Cedar Brae, where great stones broke up the river into little dams, little rapids, little whirlpools, where the children played and splashed all day long, while he and his wife sat under one of the pine trees. The hum of the factory mixers seemed far away; the happy cries of the children, the repeated bird calls, rested his nerves as they had not been rested in months. It could be a hundred miles away he told his missus. The noonday sun drew the pitch from the pine trunks, and filled his nostrils with the odor of resinous wood—just as at evening the cool, moist earth drew subtle perfume from the balm of gilead trees bordering on the woodland just across from Cedar Brae. That evening, they trudged wearily, happily homeward.

The following weekend the family returned to the valley and every weekend, weather permitting, right up until the days deep in the fall. His outings took on a different note. His wife gathered raspberries; the red, purple and black cap varieties—a few thimbleberries as well. Towards

September, they learned that some of the wild apples were quite good. Before long the shelves in his pantry at home were marking off the progress of the season by the harvest which he gathered from it.

He could talk by the hour of what he saw and the people he gradually came to know. To him the valley seemed endless; his chats with the conservation man whetted his appetite to walk the full twenty miles of this east valley of the Don. This man also told him that the two streams of the two valleys of the Don rose as springs just north of Richmond Hill. He could walk for days and not cover all of the ravines. Gradually the Green Belt was becoming a reality.

Old Tom the bird man who always seemed to be in the valley let him use, on occasion, his powerful field glasses, and nature jumped as though by magic before his eyes. The soft whistling he had heard in the meadow was the cardinal. He saw it, blood red in Old Tom's glasses and felt that he could almost touch the bird. Old Tom laughed and told him that there were hundreds of species of birds in the valley.

He met the lad who had hunted up most every wild flower in the place— 125 species right in this valley, from the yellow lady's slipper, to the fragile blue chalice of the fringed gentian. Sometimes of an evening he visited the swimming hole; discovered a second and a third one far up the valley.

There were others like himself who came to this valley for its peace and unspoiled beauty. The artists, who sat by the hour painting the scenery which hundreds of thousands of his city of a million did not know existed— and the botanists, and the nature man who imitated the whistle of most every bird, and the game wardens, and the photographers, movie cameras included and the nature teachers—all were there and many more: the Scouts, the overnight campers. Just about everybody came to the valley. Months ago it had been embalmed in his mind in the print of newspaper comments. Today it was a reality; a haven, where the hum of the factory mixers gave way to the drowsy nodding of the wind playing a harp in the pine foliage; where the honking of traffic was replaced by the cawing of the crow, the screech of brakes by the strident cry of the jay. A place where a clean stream caressed his children's feet.

Two incidents that summer put his loyalty to the valley to the test. Towards mid-August he heard chopping. Making his way to the spot he saw two lads. two hatchets and the mangled remains of what had been a fine cedar grove. For a moment he saw red—a fine beauty spot ruined. He made sure that he got the right addresses, then from his home called their parents. He told his story of what the valley meant to him, what it could mean to thousands more, and the parents understood. There would be no more chopping, but the cedar trees which were growing before he was born were gone forever.

The very next week, he took his family to a place called Watson's Park. There was a swimming hole there. He had thought of the lovely little setting all week. Then when he arrived there, he could scarcely believe his eyes. Where he had planned to sit and read, a load of garbage and refuse had been dumped. It was a form of excreta, a hundred things considered as old and useless; pipes, boxes, cans, papers, boots—everything. He was about to turn sadly away, when a thought struck him. He searched the garbage and found an envelope. The address was there alright; by sheer coincidence it was on his street. He knew the man. He put the envelope in his pocket. That night he made a call. On occasions such as this he had no polish, but he must have been convincing. The next evening the two men proceeded to the spot and cleaned up the mess, and took the junk to a regulation city dump. The next week two families, his and the other man's, spent their Sunday by the stream and a new convert to the valley had been made.

Just before Christmas he opened his morning paper and read of plans for the conservation of the valley. He set the paper down, went to a cupboard, removed a jar of black raspberry jam, which came from the valley, smeared his toast with it and began to read carefully every line. *'Don Valley Authority'*, *'Department of Planning and Development'*, *'Conservation Association'*, *'Green Belt'*. Every word stood out in his mind backed by reality. *'Green Belt'*, he muttered, 'It's more of a Life Belt, that is what it has been to me. I wonder to how many more?'

Winter 1951

Uncle Eric's Christmas Tree

LITTLE CURLY-HAIRED JAMIE lived with his Uncle Eric and Aunt Ivy in a cottage in the Don Valley, whose timbers groaned when the wind moaned, whose frame basked purringly in the hot July sun, whose roof slept snugly beneath a thick blanket of snow during the deep cold days of winter.

Now, Uncle Eric loved to do three things; he loved to live in the Don Valley; he loved to see everything in the valley, and he loved to stuff his corn-cob pipe with tobacco and puff and puff as he walked slowly along, at any time of the year, and studied every little creature, plant or flower.

One morning, a few days before Christmas, Uncle Eric stuffed his pipe with tobacco and stuffed his hiking bag with the most unheard of things; bits of string, ribbon, pieces of suet, stale bread, cobs of corn, pumpkin, citron, squash, and sunflower seeds; all from last summer's garden.

Tapping the tobacco in his pipe with his thumb as he did over and over again, and puffing each time he lit another match, he said to Aunt Ivy: *'Jamie wants me to set up a Christmas tree for the little furry folk and winter birds and I haven't the heart to disappoint him.'* So off they went, hand in hand, on the river ice; the little curly-haired boy and a tall blue-eyed man who loved the valley and puffed at his pipe as he hiked along. They strolled past the place where Uncle Eric fished in the summer; past the place where old Joe cut dead wood for his winter fuel; past the place where the hermit lived in a shack he had made himself, keeping a few goats and chickens for company; past the 'clay banks' swimming hole, then sound asleep and dreaming of the boys it would entertain next summer; past the sugar bush where *'black-mask'* the raccoon lived. Along ever so many twists and turns until they reached Juniper hill, perched high above the river on a slope of the valley. Many a time Uncle Eric had come out here alone, to sit by a great campfire in deep contentment, and always putting to sleep every little spark of the fire afterwards.

Pushing little Jamie up the steep slope, Uncle Eric came to his favourite ledge which commanded a wide view of the valley and of the river. He made a little fire to keep them warm, then walked across the ledge to a nice looking hemlock tree and said that it would be their live Christmas tree. He knew this hemlock well, stroked its branches, sniffed its odorous needles, which pleased the hemlock ever so much. *'We're going to pretty you up no end,'* he said. So he took the pieces of string and ribbon and tied all of the suet, the bread, apple cores and cobs of corn to the branches. The seeds which Uncle Eric brought along were scattered in the clefts of the hemlock's strong arms. He scattered many things about the frozen ground as well; even a few carrots as a special treat for the little brown bunnies of the woods.

Little Jamie and Uncle Eric thrilled with pleasure when they saw what they had accomplished. Then they returned to the fire, and boiled water for hot chocolate, and ate the sandwiches which Aunt Ivy had put up for them. *'Jamie,'* said Uncle Eric, *'I hope old 'black mask', the raccoon, has sense enough to crawl out of that deep hole away down in the trunk of the big sugar maple, back in the sugar bush, and get this corn. The birds will be around soon enough. Here come some chickadees, and I fancy I heard a cardinal back in the woods there. The jays are sounding their little tin horns, just like they do back at the cottage. There will be a feast around here soon enough.'* Uncle Eric puffed at his pipe a while and told Jamie stories of the woods, which the little boy loved to hear. By and by they walked hand in hand down the frozen stream, past all the old familiar landmarks, back to the little cottage which stood above the river bank. Inside the house everything was so home-like and cosy; even to the blocks of pine in the wood stove which sent blue smoke curling up the chimney to perfume the sharp winter air. That night, while the cradle of a half-moon rocked itself over the horizon, little Jamie twisted and rolled in his sleep long long into the darkness, and until his little bed wondered what was the matter with him. *'He's dreaming about the Christmas tree,'* said Uncle Eric as he talked to Aunt Ivy, puffed at his pipe, poked at the bowl with his fingers, and lit match after match, while the fire in the big wood stove settled down to a sleep of its own, wrapped in a blanket of hot ashes.

A few days after Christmas, Uncle Eric rambled up to Juniper hill alone. *'Just to check up on the critters,'* he said. He knew that they had been there alright. Nothing but the ribbon and the string remained. But as he stroked the hemlock tree's foliage and sniffed the camphor odor of its branches, he noticed a piece of writing paper hanging from one of them. This is what he read:

"His heart was full of love and good will,
for the little creatures on Juniper hill.
Tomorrow is Christmas they must have their tree.
I won't hang a stocking but good things there'll be.
So Uncle Eric wended his way to the crest,
Selected a tree prepared for the rest.
With string from his pocket and morsels to suit,
he tied to the branches choice suet and fruit.
Then bread and soft pork; what pleasured they bring.
The birds and the creatures his praises will sing:
Nightfall its blanket of calm and repose;
little eyes peering from woodland abode,
eyes filled with wonder, surprise and content;
furry bodies towards the Christmas tree bent:
Next day at dawn, the pheasants, the cardinal, the jay
their Christmas through Uncle Eric made bright and gay.'

'I wonder who wrote that stuff,' mused Uncle Eric. *'Let's see, there are boot prints in the snow leading off through those pine woods. No time to follow the trail now.'* And with that, Uncle Eric scattered more pumpkin and sunflower seeds around the hemlock, stuffed his pipe with tobacco and followed the frozen stream homeward.

Away up the valley, *'Old Tom'* the bird man was out on one of his many bird hikes. He had a fire of his own, and as he sat by it and steeped his tea, he thought of the note in the hemlock tree, and chuckled and chuckled and chuckled.

Spring 1952

Sweet Maple Water

'SAP'S RUNNING!' These words proclaim an awakening; the quickening of nature's pulse; the birth of a new season; the last harvest of winter; the first harvest of spring.

Ever tap a maple tree? You drill a hole about one inch deep in the trunk of the tree about two feet from the ground. You hammer in a sap spout and to it hang a pail. On a bright frosty late March morning, having done these things, you will see a first bead of water, pushed impetuously forward by other beads of maple sap anxious to be free. These drops of water strike the pail with a rhythmic 'dot, dip,tinkle,tinkle;' just like a leaking tap. An hour or so later you will have your first quaff of maple water.

Are you a little more venturesome? Fill several pails with sap. When you have a gallon or so, set it on your kitchen stove and let it boil until reduced to a small quantity of syrup. How much? Well, it takes from thirty-five to forty gallons of sap water to make a gallon of syrup. But even a small quantity makes you feel that you are doing something which white men have done in this country since the early years of its settlement, and the Indians before them: you are toasting the season; you are greeting it; you are savoring of it.

We know, of course, that the maple syrup industry is a big one; it turns, literally speaking, the maple woods of Ontario and of Quebec into millions of dollars of syrup, retailing at about six dollars a gallon. But, we back-fence 'producers' just do the thing for fun. One spring I made seven gallons of syrup with several friends. We worked like fury, carrying the sap in five gallon containers from way across the valley, and all for one gallon of maple syrup each. But you cannot buy the thrill of stepping out into the early morning sunshine, on a slope covered with maple trees, while the crows caw and the sap drops merrily into the pails. Nor can you buy the thrill of maple water boiling and sizzling in the big pan in the shed; or the adventure of keeping the stove company long long into the night, when everything is asleep but the agitated water becoming more syrup-like with each passing hour. Nor can you buy this product of the woods just like you made it. It is your syrup, perhaps from your own trees.

'The hushed quiet of March woods.

Moonlight shimmering on the clear sweet water in the pails.'

The hard maple is the best tree for syrup sap; a massive column of wood;

31

The sugar cabin of W.F.MacLean in its heyday. It was known to hundreds of boys in the early 1920's. Today not a vestige remains. The MacLean sugar bush stood in the east valley of the Don on a line with Eglinton Avenue, if extended easterly.

bark tawny brown; a cathedral pillar of the woods; the home of the raccoon; rock of ages. Water exudes more slowly from this species of maple; its sugar content is higher, hence its name sugar maple. The sugar maple is one of the tallest of Canadian hardwoods, reaching to 130 feet. It is often seen in the Don Valley four feet in diameter. Because the hard maple is a really valuable commercial tree, 'sugar bush stands' are unfortunately sacrificed in some instances for this reason.

All other maples will give sap from which syrup can be made. The soft maple of our woods, and town and city streets, flows abundantly when tapped. Its syrup is good, although the sugar content of the water is less than that of the true sugar maple. Even the sap of the weedy Manitoba maple will make syrup.

Since the early days of the settlement of the Don Valley, maple syrup has been made along its stretches. To this day, hundreds of its giant sugar maples could still be tapped, although people no longer depend on them as a sole source of table sugar. They are now ours to be preserved as reminders of the primeval forest.

'A hot sun and frosty night causes the sap to run most. Slits are cut in the bark of the trees and wooden troughs set under the trees into which the sap, a clear sweet water, runs.' That was in 1794, when the sap was boiled in large kettles over an open fire. Taffy was made by pouring the syrup on the snow. Cakes of sugar were secured through long boiling—welcome indeed in a new land where sugar was almost unobtainable.

Does it harm maple trees to tap them? What is the best time to make maple syrup? These are the usual questions asked. A young tree should not be tapped for too many successive years. In the case of a mature tree, the incision will close over in a season or two and no harm results; the sap collected from the treee is veritably a mere drop in the bucket. The time for tapping trees depends on the season. Warm days following sharp nights from about mid-March to early April is the usual time for the Toronto area. The sap is temperamental and sometimes does not run when we think it should. It will run in February on a warm day.

There are several popular notions concerning the discovery that maple sap would make maple syrup. The settlers saw the Indians boiling the sap and were delighted with the result. We fancy, however, that nature made the secret an open one: an obvservant rambler will notice a sticky substance adhering to the bark of a maple tree, where the wind broke one of its branches during the winter. By March the sap begins to run; the sun cooks the thin stream of water; a primitive practice of syrup making, probably the first of all, and handed down to us to this day.

Spring 1952

The Don: Floods, Fish, Freshets, Flotsam

SHOULD THE WINTER BE LONG AND COLD, the river ice will hold until mid-March or a week or two later. Then, usually, during a warm rain, the ice will begin to crack, heave and shove in the centre of the stream: the drive is on. Quietly at first, then with increased momentum, huge blocks of ice from two to three feet thick move out like an army in retreat. Abandoned floes strew the shoreline. Two days later, the river is free once more. Should the winter be mild with occasional freeze-ups, the ice may break once a month. Accordingly, the floes will be a few inches thick only.

The usual flood level of the Don is about six feet above summer surface—more, should a heavy rainfall occur at the exact time of the break-up, or should the snow melt rapidly. No two floods will be exactly alike. One year there was no flood; just a quiet rotting away of the ice where the frozen roots of winter had been moulded months before. In the summer which followed this miscarriage in nature's plans, the river was full of weeds. There have been some great floods on the Don. On April 4th, 1850, the

The ice begins to crack and heave in the centre of the river. Two days later, a few blocks only remain, to tell of the break-up.

---

two bridges which, at that time, spanned the Don were carried away by a rampaging river of unprecedented proportions. This flood was caused by the rapid melting of snow along the headwaters of the Don.

But by far the worst Don flood was that of September 14, 1878. It was referred to as 'the great rainstorm'; a tribute to a rainfall of ·diluvial proportions. All five bridges on the Don were swept away: the Taylor bridge crashed into the Gerrard Street bridge. In the wake of the floating bridge, came furniture, trees, remnants of barns, chicken coops, framework of saw mills. At King and Queen Streets the scene was one of desolation. Water reached several hundreds of feet beyond each bank of the Don. Finally the bridge at Queen Street gave way and went careening down towards the bay. This flood destroyed most of the old mills on the Don. There have been other floods: 'In the spring—during the so-called freshets, the Don became a swirling tide reaching across the whole vale, carrying wrecks of fences, sheds, carcasses of sheep and other farm stock.' In our time most everyone has seen blocks of ice lying along the railway tracks skirting the banks of the lower Don.

All floods on the Don are of short duration. The watershed of the east and west Don rivers is about twenty miles along in each instance. This area drains all water eventually converging into the two Don rivers. The strength of flood water is divided until it reaches the 'forks', only three miles from the bay. Building on the watershed has an effect on floods; storm sewers carry into the stream water which formerly soaked into the land.

The Don, frozen over, was always a picturesque stream. 'There is a great deal of snow on the river Don,' wrote Mrs. Simcoe on January 14, 1794. 'It was so well frozen that we walked some miles upon it today.' And, again on February 3, 1796: 'We drove on the ice to Skinner's Mill—a mile beyond Castle Frank—At the mouth of the Don, I fished from my carriole, but the fish are not to be caught as they were last winter, several dozen in an hour.'—'Our driving over the ice frightens way the fish.'

The Don, frozen and with a coating of snow, reminded Dr. Scadding, whose father came over with the Simcoes, of a level English coach road. Instead of the rotting row of cedar piles which today line the Don at Queen Street, the river was bordered on each side by 'wild willow, alder. wychhazel, dogwood and tree cranberry.' 'In winter, the solidly frozen stream was utilized in preference to the surrounding roads.'

'Down the river thus conveniently paved over, every day came a cavalcade of strong sleighs, heavily laden some with cordwood, some with sawn lumber, some with hay, southerly towards the Bay.' 'The lofty and steep hillsides along the stream clothed in deep snow presented very picturesque winter scenery.' 'Southward a great stretch of marsh with the blue lake on the horizon.'

For generations the frozen Don was used by thousands of skaters, who, of a Sunday afternoon, covered the ice with their moving forms. In the memory of many persons living today are such scenes to be recalled.

A letter from George Playter to Commissary McGill indicates that the Don of 1796 or thereabouts was put to another practical use: 'Sergeant Lyndan informed me thou art desirous I should sled some boards from Skinner's Mill to Castle Frank. If I do, thou must pay me one quarter of a dollar for every hundred feet not exceeding one inch thick.'

Today, the upper Don is still picturesque. A walk along the river ice is an adventure in eye photography for the scenery-searching hiker. The serpentine course of the stream, opening out into new vistas, is a veritable nature movie. Every few hundred yards or so there is a tiny rapids. It is here that one sees evidence of the skill of the frost king's fingers. In these open places, water splashing against the encompassing ice has fashioned along its edges foliage, or call it ice vegetation, or ice beards, pipe organs or just plain icicles. There are also bells of ice, shaped unmistakably so, moulded and suspended one after the other from a ledge of ice, somewhat as a chime against which the hurrying water strikes up its own tinkling tune. Elsewhere the ice has been brushed lightly over the water. Seen through this transparent cover, the river becomes a veritable aquarium; a tiny, sheltered sea bottom, a sanctuary of hibernation for all it contains. Occasionally an offshoot of a rapids will glide away on its own, along the shallow river shoreline; squeezing itself between the sandy bottom and the ice immediately above it; darting along as so many blobs of quicksilver; a thing alive.

No river is complete without its fish or fish stories: the Don is no
exception. Where the General Steel Wares Plant now stands, the Don made
a curve in what was known as the great bend. Dr. Scadding relates how it
was his habit to sit on a sandy cliff on this bend and to gaze down into the
waters of the river, where on a sunny day he could discern in the stream
shoals of sun fish and the form of a pike or two lurking in the shadows.

'The Indians (January 17,1794) have cut holes in the ice over which they
spread blankets on poles and they sit under the shed, moving a wooden fish
hung to a line in the water by way of attracting the living fish.' Mrs. Simcoe
also tells of fishing for red trout through holes in the ice of the Don. In a
later day an 'old boy' of 1850 tells of the good fishing in Taylor's Mill race.
Many a large string of perch, bass, sun fish and chub were carried home to
Yorkville and peddled through the streets. 'Mud Creek' which runs through
North Rosedale ravine was full of shiners, chub and soldier fish, so named
because of a red stripe along each side.

The salmon were plentiful in the Don. Dr. Scadding saw as many as
twenty heavy salmon speared within an hour. 'In the latter part of the
summer,' writes William Lea, 'the finest salmon were taken in great
quantities sometimes weighing twenty-five pounds each.' 'Good fish of
other kinds beside the salmon were numerous,' to again quote Dr. Scadding;
'black bass, rock bass, perch, pike. Spring water rivulets entering the main
stream at several points were frequented by speckled trout.' Middleton adds
another note of nostalgia to the past fame of the Don: 'Trout took the fly
eagerly in the season and all kinds of fish were caught in winter by lines
dropped though holes in the ice. Sawdust in the streams drove away the
game fish but the long suffering mullet or sucker persisted. To this day
schools of 'suckers' crowd the river at the time of the spring freshet and the
juvenile of 1923, even as his great grandfather in the days of his youth, goes
fishing with a bushel-and-a-half basket under his arm and a scoop shovel on
his shoulder.'

'The water in front of the dam at the lower Taylor Mill', relates Mr. Jim
Lea, 'was a cauldron of fish.' 'They were gatherd by the wagon load and fed
to the hogs.' Catfish were caught by the tubfull in the lower Don between
Queen Street and Riverdale Park.

As recently as April, 1925, Owen Staples, then well-known Toronto
artist, wrote: 'The suckers are abundant in our lakes and rivers and even in
marshes and ponds. They spawn in early spring soon after the ice goes out,
when they force their way up the swollen river and through the rapids to
gravelly beds. The flesh is firm and eatable at this time.' Even twenty years
ago, the banks of the Don, by Pottery Road, were white with the forms of
stranded suckers.

There are still fish of a kind in the Don. Carp are caught in the east Don,
weighing seven to ten pounds each. Shiners are in multitude. There are
some trout, 'escapees' from the stocked ponds of the headwaters of the Don;
even a few goldfish, dumped into the stream by cottagers. Alas, the

surviving fish are fighting a foot-by-foot rear guard action against elimination. Whenever branches of the Don become polluted, the fish move farther along towards the headwaters.

Close to a large centre of population, the Don has always had its appeal to the small fry, who each spring and summer line its banks equipped with home-made fishing lines and poles. The most colourful fisherman on the Don was one 'Catfish Joe.' Ernest Thompson Seton refers to him as a singular character, a respectable Englishman who went native on a low island at the mouth of the Don. 'His chief joy was fishing and his chief reliance among the finnies was the catfish. Hence the name.'

There are still inveterate fishermen on the Don; some men and a few birds and animals as well. The kingfisher is a brother fisherman-in-feathers. He plunges from a perch fifty feet above the water and has the vision to see at that distance a fish three inches long. All summer and fall and during an occasional winter as well, the kingfisher's rattle is heard along the Don. The bird delights in minnows, chub, crawfish and frogs.

Sometimes one will hear the low, hoarse croak of a crane or blue heron and see its motionless, hunch-backed form standing by the river shore. A flash of the long bill and a small fish disappears down the heron's gullet. This reminder of the stork now winters with us. The bittern, a member of the same family, is another fisherman of the Don.

And there is the mink: 'small fish are perhaps his preferred food and he delights in taking them by open pursuit.' By a hole in the ice in the lower Don a mink pulled a one pound fish from the water, then hurried off when alarmed by the approach of a man and a dog.

These little episodes of still existing wild life are enacted every day in season, a stone's throw from the pulsating traffic artery of Don Mills Road—a portrait of conservation at our doorstep.

The course of the Don is ever changing. Figuratively speaking the river is a sieve; it washes gravel, sand, stones and clay and deposits them into separate piles; a veritable gravel pit owner. It plays a game of give and take. It erodes one bank and with its residue builds up a shore or ledge a few yards farther downstream. With the instinct of a beaver it topples over large trees against which it piles up the debris of the flood, then covers them over with silt as a turtle its eggs. Against this barrier the stream deviates its course and soon another bend is formed.

The willow is the one factor which keeps the battle of the river versus soil from being too one-sided. One would believe that the germ of willow growth is in the water itself. A tiny beach of sand left in the wake of the receding flood reveals in June, hundreds of tiny willow rootlets. A few years later they have grown sufficiently to become a trap for the ice floes and a sieve for debris-laden waters.

Adjoining the east Don river are large, marshy, spring-fed ponds. They mark the original course of the river prior to the laying of the Canadian National Railways line up the valley. These ponds are seats of conservation for aquatic life; the convention hall of frogs and turtles; the building lots of muskrats; the meeting place of brown ducks in increasing numbers.

Summer 1952

Wild Fruit

IN THE DON VALLEY are found all of the bush and ground fruits of the Ontario countryside. There are red, purple and black raspberries; the blackberry or thimbleberry; the small wild strawberry; the elderberry; red and black currants; the blueberry; the gooseberry and wild grapes. There are several varieties of wild cherry including pin and choke cherries. In the fields grow the ground cherry and in the woods the mandrake or maple apple. These are the wild fruits we are likely to find on a summer or fall ramble.

The season of wild fruit begins with the ripening of the succulent strawberry. It grows in abundance, dotting the meadows with tiny patches of red fruit, usually towards the end of June. About mid-July the first red raspberries ripen, large and juicy in the lowlands, firm and round on the slopes. The purple raspberry, less abundant, is usually seen growing along with the red variety. The black raspberry or 'black cap' bears heavily on wooded slopes. The fruit is firm, easy to pick, obviously seedy. The canes remain in bearing for at least three weeks, a few berries ripening each day.

The blueberry, although generally associated with the late summer of the highlands of Ontario, is ready for picking in the Don Valley about the first of July. There are a few colonies of this bush fruit growing along the crests of the valley. They do not bear profusely; each patch yields several quarts of good-tasting fruit.

The May apple has ripened by August. It is edible and can be used to make marmalade and jelly. The juice can be added to lemonade and other fruit drinks: the root is poisonous. The ground cherry also ripens by mid-summer. The wild cherries are anything but delectable to most people; their virtue lies in the fine jellies fo which they are the base. The red and black currants adds a touch of the garden to our cavalcade of wild fruit. 'Swamp' red currant is found in three wild species along with a few kinds also from the garden. It is said that the red currant is host plant for the white pine blister rust.

The gooseberry, a native plant, grows almost to the artic circle. It is common and abundant in the Don Valley.

The blackberry or thimbleberry, as it is commonly called, is queen of the late bush fruits. If you can brave its thorns, the blackberry is well worth the effort. The fruit is large and juicy, somewhat seedy; excellent for jam.

September has its special fruit, the elderberry. We are all familiar with its large clumps of fruit to which adhere hundreds of small, round, purple berries; good equally for wine, jelly or jam. The elderberry is now used commercially in blends with apple products. It spreads easily from root cuttings, and provides abundant food for birds. Flickers and robins delight in its fruit.

During the first week of October a late variety of wild red raspberry yields profusely in the valley and ends the harvest of bush fruits for the year. With the advent of late October, small blue grapes are seen hanging from vines amidst the changing leaves of the lowlands.

Wild fruits are an embellishment of the season; a ration for the hiker; thirst quenchers on a hot summer day. They are also a potential supply of delicious jams and jellies.

The hardy adventurers who term themselves pickers of wild fruit earn every little fruit globule they gather. Theirs is the way of hill and dale, bog and marsh, meadow and woodland, mosquito and gnat. In season, they are to be seen in wide brim straw hats, basket in hand, moving slowly from bush to bush, from patch to patch. They brave the flies and the heat, the showers and the thunderstorms, the brambles and the thorns. To a real fruit picker it is just fun. Sometimes they are rewarded in an extravagant manner where some combination of ideal growing conditions produces raspberries of enormous size and abundance. Then they gather many many quarts quickly and easily.

To these fruit pickers, winter days have a pleasant beginning with a breakfast of toast smeared with delicious wild raspberry jam or elderberry jelly; the harvest of many a summer day has matured in the preserves on their shelves.

Where there is fruit, wild or tame, there are also birds. Is it fair to say that they pilfer our strawberries, raspberries, and cherries? To the bird this fruit is merely an unaccountable gratuity of nature, which has augmented over the years the store of the wild varieties.

We do not pay much attention nowadays to the wild fruit of the countryside. When the country was first settled, however, wild fruit was the only fruit store to which grandma could go. The settlers tell many a tale of their fruit gathering excursions and worked out ingenious ways of preserving the fruit they gathered.

Next time you are able to do so, gather a little wild fruit, sufficient even for one or two jars of jam or jelly. It will bind the fine days of summer even closer to you. It will be your way of tasting of the Canadian countryside. Perhaps you may be able to bring in a dish of wild raspberries to the farm house where you are staying. There you will pour rich country cream over the fruit, with perhaps just a dash of honey for sweetening: try it sometime.

The Ghost of Storkey's Well

'WE'LL SET THE HOUSE HERE MA *and we'll try for the well over there, that wet spot; looks like a por.'* So old Storkey went to work—on the well and then the cabin, turn about, for he needed both. He dug down into the pore as he called it; one, two, three feet, the soil getting wetter all the time; then to six feet, with plenty of water. He wasn't sure after that how deep the water was, for a pole rammed through the sand did not touch bottom. He closed in the hole with a wooden frame; the water came close to the top. *'That's the water supply,'* he said, and so it was, throughout the years that old Storkey ate out his heart and his strength on those hummocks which he once called a farm.

The pine forest looked good when he first saw it; magnificent scenery which he hacked down and dragged away a log at a time to the saw mill on the stream a few miles from his holdings. He needed wheat and 'taters' most; wood next. So he got rid of the wood as fast as he could; first the logs and then the stumps. Some he had pulled, some rotted away. Then over the years the soil which he had cleared stood out like an island risen from the bottom of the sea of pine verdure which once covered it.

For a few years, things seemed alright. The forest had manured the soil for centuries, so why should he, then again with what? So the wheat grew and the potatoes and a few other things as well.

A few years more, and his soil a little 'thread bare' started to peter out; his hummocks were turning to blow sand. On windy days he chewed sand, spit it out of his mouth, rubbed it out of his eyes, cursed it. It seemed then, the life had gone out of the farm. The sand was like oil, spreading, ever spreading down the slopes, along the flat land. Only the well was good, and the acre about it; that one spot of green; 'the only good thing on the place" Storkey said, the day he, Ma and the kids packed up and beat it for the lakeshore settlement. That was in 1880.

Ed Landman knew nothing of old Storkey on that day in May in 1927 when he and a planting crew came along to the hummocks. Ed had it all figured out. It was part of a project; two million trees for this area, and how it needed it. Ed had lain awake winter nights thinking of those hummocks. He'd get his poplars and locusts on the ridges. They would grip on to anything, most anything. That would hold the sand against any wind. And the pines; he would plant them closer to the bottom of the slopes—the kind that grew three feet in a season—scotch pine; then later, red pine.

The crew planted all morning, and the trees were set in the sand by the thousands. Ed spied a patch of green—wandered over to have a look; took a few steps; started suddenly to drop through a void; made a quick grab at a poplar; barked his shins; saved himself from the rotten frame. Ed knew now it was a well.

Noon time he called the men over. They had a good look. It was a well of any farmer's dreams. Lots of water, sweet and cold as ice. A miracle; a heart beat where most tree life had died.

After hours Ed came back with a few volunteers from the crew. They cleaned out the old well, took up the rotting boards and set them aside reverently, like the bones of some old pioneer. They built a new frame, and a top four feet above ground. One of the men had a pump and a length of pipe. It was a neat affair when finished and the water poured out sweet, cold and abundant.

Years later the poplars and the locusts of Ed's planting, had grown into tall trees, weaving their roots into the sand and holding it in a grip that almost strangled it. The pines grew tall, some as bushy as a palm tree. They grew close to the well, where now people came to drink.

In town one day, Ed looked up the records: Concession 2 lot 6 Johaida Storkey. Land taken out in 1860, abandoned in 1880. *'Poor devil'* thought Ed, *'What a time he had.'*

Fall 1952

The Don as a Source of Drinking Water

THE NAME OF THOMAS C. KEEFER, ESQ., means nothing to the citizens of Toronto today. In 1847, Keefer was the central figure of a long, and it would seem to us, unbelievable controversy. *'Could the Don produce water in sufficient quantity for the requirements of the city of Toronto?'* That was the important question of the day.

The Keefer plan dealt specifically with the west Don River and to a lesser extent with the Humber River as well. These streams, it was believed, could make available 24 million cubic feet of water daily. Storage tanks would be employed and water from them would reach the city through the gravitation system. Today the Keefer report is almost unknown—only one copy of it remains in the Toronto City Hall Library. As time proved, however, it paved the way for still other reports on the subject of drinking water for Toronto.

In the year 1887 Messrs. McAlpine and Tully, Civil Engineers, reported to the city council of Toronto on a proposed supply of water by gravitation from the Oak Ridges lakes, the river Don and the Rouge river. In February of the same year, Mayor Howland of Toronto stated that a supply of 20 million gallons of water could be obtained by gravitation from the headwaters of the middle and west branches of the Don at a cost of $500,000.

Why Toronto, with Lake Ontario to draw on, should consider securing water from so small a stream as the Don, is explained to some extent by Professor Laut Carpenter's allusion to the city's (then) system of pumping water from the lake. To quote Professor Carpenter: *'A town may go on for some time drinking contaminated water with apparent freedom from illness,'* (a reference to the condition of Toronto's water supply), *'The leaks from the pipes across the bay, the discoloured state of the water after heavy gales indicates that the causes of pollution have not been removed. I am convinced that the citizens have never been supplied with pure water at all seasons of the year.'*

In the month of February 1887, Messrs. McAlpine and Tully again assured Mayor Howland that an abundant supply of pure and wholesome water could be obtained from the river sources mentioned, at an annual cost of only half of the existing lake system.

The general features of the proposed gravity plan suggested that the waters from the Oak Ridges lakes could be conducted to the headwaters of the Don in steel pipes. The Oak Ridges lakes lying north of Toronto included Bond lake, Wilcox lake, Preston lake and others. The waters of the three main branches of the Don would be intercepted at an elevation of 300 feet and conveyed to the waterworks in steel pipes. Storage reservoirs would be built in suitable places in the two valleys of the Don to receive and retain excessive rainfall or excessive river water. Messrs. McAlpine and Tully went into elaborate detail to prove their point. Their findings on the subject are indeed interesting to read.

In 1887 there was much to recommend this plan. It had proved itself successful elsewhere. The position of the Don watershed favoured its application to that area. It seemed logical to put the Oak Ridges lakes to this constructive use.

In 1887 Toronto, with a population of 120,000, required twelve million gallons of water daily. It was foreseen that this demand might even increase to thirty million gallons daily. 'The construction of the necessary works for diverting the waters of the west, middle and east branches of the Don would supply twenty-five million gallons per day to the Rosehill reservoir.' It was further specified that the flow from the middle and east branches of the Don could be diverted to a reservoir below Thornhill, then conveyed in a steel pipe to the Rosehill Reservoir. To dispel fears as to the purity of the

Patterson Pond on a branch of the East Don River, was made in 1840 to supply water power for a grist mill; average depth, eleven feet. *Photo courtesy: W. Redelmeier, proprietor, Don-Head Farms, Richmond Hill, Ontario.*

water obtained from these branches of the river Don, McAlpine and Tully made this statement: *'If the water supply from north of Toronto is objectionable on account of supposed pollution from farmyards, farm houses, outbuildings, villages and graveyards, how much more objectionable the waters of Lake Ontario which are a natural reservoir for pollution of all kinds, etc.'* There followed in the report a long and detailed explanation of the purity of water 'oxidized' by contact with the atmosphere, running through streams self-purified.

The reservoirs on the Don would have been completed one year following acceptance of the McAlpine and Tully project. The plan, however, disappeared into the oblivion of deliberation; Toronto continued to get its water supply from Lake Ontario. The feasability of securing drinking water from the Don, once in the print of two reports gradually faded from the public eye. Drinking water for Toronto then entered the Lake Simcoe stage; a project which, in 1891, ran high in possibilities: Lake Simcoe, it was stated, offered Toronto a natural and everlasting reservoir which could be made available without dams.

Late in 1890, Messrs. McLellan, Stuart and Chapman, Civil Engineers, made a survey to estimate the cost of bringing Lake Simcoe water to Toronto. The grandiose scheme of canals, tunnel and electric power development assigned to the Don an important role: *'One of the principal points for developing this power will be at the crossing of the river Don into which stream it is proposed to pass all of the water not required in the city at present, the effect of which will increase the current in the Don which would be sufficient to thoroughly scour it out and remove all the filth and pollution which now make the river so objectionable as regards public health.'*

These words picture the Don as a turbulent 'mountain stream' of Lake Simcoe water, swirling and churning its way through the East Don Valley with the rapidity of a spring freshet; the delight of the anglers, the fascination of hikers, the dream of dreamers. Obviously the remarks concerning the Don as an objectionable stream, referred in 1890 to that section only of the river which flowed through the city. Even today the East Don above the forks of the Don is still a clean stream.

The project to bring water from Lake Simcoe to Toronto included a canal to be made by the Georgian Bay Canal Company and the Georgian Bay Ship Canal and Power Aqueduct Company. At the fever pitch of the discussion James Mansergh, Civil Engineer of Westminster, England, was brought to Toronto to report fully on the situation of Toronto water. This he did in a scathing denouncement of all projects concerning Lake Simcoe gravitation, the Oak Ridges lakes, the Don, Humber and Rouge rivers.

'After a full consideration of this proposal, (Lake Simcoe) *I unhesitatingly condemn it.'* Mr. Mansergh also lashed out at the sewage system of the day. *'To discharge all of the sewage of a hundred and seventy-five thousand people in its crude state into a tideless and practically stagnant harbour is obviously a very wrong thing to do and every rational man must condemn it.'*

And what of the Don today? From the lofty pinnacle of Toronto's greatest engineering dreams of the latter part of the 19th century, the lower Don has descended to the level of a sludge laden, oily surfaced sluggish stream, tainted with the offal of factories and the effluent of several sewage disposal plants. Concerning this water we read:

'The effluent from the North Toronto Sewage Treatment Works discharges into the river above Todmorden. But it is a fact that the effluent from this modern and efficient plant actually is considerably purer in form than the river water with which it mixes and has the effect to clarify it.'

This can be considered as sheer satire, considering the already polluted state of the waters of the Don where they reach the North Toronto plant.

Should anyone take seriously the statement as to the purity of the water from disposal plants along the Don, that person is invited to spend a few moments at their outlet pipes. What a contrast with the sewage free, clear spring waters of the upper Don where it murmurs peacefully and poetically over the river stones much the same way as in the pioneer days of this country.

At times a discharge of dye into the Don gives the stream, as it flows

44

under the Toronto bridges, the appearance of an oblong vat of pigment. Where people once rowed boats in the summer or skated on the ice in winter, the sole surviving traffic now consists of a derelict log or a floating tentacular root stump. Even the most vulgar of fish have long since abandoned these waters; truly a foul-smelling open sewer.

An old timer is of the opinion that Keating's cut merely served to back up the Don water as far north as Bloor Street. Before the cut was made the Don was scoured out at least once a year by Nature.

Beautiful Silver Creek, alias Taylor or Scarboro Creek, although silvery at its source, smells nauseatingly as it pours its fetid effluent-laden waters into those of the East Don. The West Don is polluted along most of its course. Only the snug little brooks of the headwaters of the Don watershed seem safe and secure. Already 'projects' are appraising the effluent carrying qualities of the East Don river, still a clean stream.

The Don no longer fits into the city's plans for drinking water (that belongs to the romantic past). It is appraised today as a sewer and the chief concern is how much more sewage can it carry?

Fall 1952

Mac's Acres Go Back to the Woodland

MAC HAD BOUGHT THE THIRTY-TWO ACRES five years before. The cleared part of his purchase stretched in a long strip, bordered on one side by woodland; on the other side by the railway track. This strip was broken up by two ponds and their marshy consorts, an area which was considered with some optimism as suitable for a truck garden. It was the home of the Redwinged blackbird, the Willow-herb and the Elecampane when Mac took over.

With much patience and considerable work, he subjugated the wild crops of his holdings and aspired to his own crop. He channelled the brook and so dried up the marsh. He drove the blackbirds away or rather they left of their own accord for other realms of bulrushes and reedy shores. On this reclaimed land he grew cucumbers, potatoes and squash and fought many a weary battle with the new seeds of old weeds which seemed to be always of the soil; they were as rash on its face which somehow he could not quite dispel; a form of revolt against his ownership. He almost drained the pond and caused the ancient turtles to scuttle to the distant river for new water.

In the back field as he called it, he planted corn; I passed that way the summer after Mac had given up the fight: *"Twasn't any use,'* he said. He couldn't battle them all, including the raccoons which at night stealthily

45

stole his cobs and the ground hogs which nibbled at his cabbages. The corn stalks of the year before, dried and tattered, hung in long lines like the rags of the uniforms of a battle-weary regiment, already half-submerged in the tempestuous waves of new weeds.

Mac had manured the soil and in this opulence the Fireweed and the wild Aster grew as they had never grown before. The rustle of the decaying corn stalks mingled with the sad note of a breeze in the pine foliage from the nearby fence line. Everywhere tiny seedling trees crept across the field as an Iroquois war party towards Mac's beaten furrows; soon no thing of the garden would grow in their shade. In the lower acres, where Mac's plow had once ripped open the black, moisture-laden muck, the mounded indented land wore a tight jacket of small weeds, as profuse as grass—all of the epitaph that Mac's graveyard of a garden needed.

The Red-winged blackbird is back, nesting once more in the marshland which time has also restored. The stalks of the Willow-herb purse new flowering cups in an invitation to the honey-bee. The Jewelweed, the Elecampane, the Vervain, all are there, just as they were when Mac took over. The turtles again brush the surface of the lazy pond, which seepage has brought to its former level. The frogs trill away the quiet hours of May and June, watching the swallows skim close to the water.

And the disgruntled raccoon, come nightfall, shuffles through the empty fields of the back acres, pulling at the tattered old corn foliage, searching the empty field for fresh cobs. Only the rhubarb remains. Choked in weeds, abandoned, it noses its long leathery roots deeper and deeper into the black soil. It is only a matter of months, when it too will be buried under; Mac's acres have gone back to the woodland.

Fall 1952

Old Black Mask - A Lovable Creature

ON A RAINY EVENING IN JUNE, something, it proved to be a furry body, dropped from out of the foliage of an apple tree and strolled across the veranda. It was a raccoon; at home, a stone's throw from a city street.

The raccoon, once a denizen of the deeper woodlands near Toronto, once hunted almost to extinction, is now staging a 'come-back'. He is heard, is often seen by almost every resident living on or near the Don Valley. At times he has even strolled downtown to win for himself a place in the day's news. He rummages in garbage pails with the familiarity of a house cat; he is a lovable, mischievous addition to our near-to-home wildlife.

Along the Don Valley, he is taking over, in increasing numbers, the big deep holes of the hollow maple and basswood trees. He forages at night for crawfish, toads and such like in the streams. He has been known to raid hen roosts at night. He finds corn delectable.

What are the habits of this member of the bear family? The corn or hens which he may take are far surpassed by the services he renders to man, because of the mice, beetles, rats and moles which the raccoon destroys. His diet also includes insects, frogs, even wild grapes.

The footprint which looks like a miniature human hand mark, shows where the coon has foraged, particularly on moonlight nights—a time for hunting which he prefers to all others. You may see him on just such nights, his eager eyes and black mask with a surrounding ring of white, pulling some choice morsel from the water, carefully washing it before eating it. He is the very soul of mischief; if tamed will take a toll of whatever comes within his reach in the household.

'Mama' coon bears from four to six young coons about mid-April. The family hibernates during the severe part of the winter, usually in a high hollow part of a tree. The fur of the raccoon is thick, long and pepper and salt grey; the tail is ringed with black.

The Don Valley was always the home of the raccoon. It boasted once of the presence of Chris Stong, the greatest coon hunter of all time, according to Stong. In the twenty years preceding January 1906, Stong took 2,541 coons in the immediate vicinity of Toronto. In the winter of 1902-3 he took 167. Stong could read a coon tree like a book. He could tell immediately of there was a coon or coons in it. He knew that coons prefer to go up a tree adjacent to the one they live in, proving there is a limb to cross over on.

The natural increase in coons, according to Stong philosophy, depended on the number of trees suitable as dens. Stong never cut down a coon tree. 'The true coon hunter,' he observed, 'practised conservation in this respect and had an eye for the future.'

Stong invented a spur for climbing. He also designed a rope to go about the tree and a belt and shoulder harness to go about his body. He literally walked up coon trees. Stong was well versed in his work; he knew exactly where to cut a hole, put in his hand, grab a coon and thrown him down to the ground to his dog.

Stong took most of his coons in December, January and February when they were denned up for the winter. A coon, he said, can go for weeks without food. The claws of the coon are his great defense. Stong also said that the coon does not call but has a sort of 'Chop-Bubble'. Stong's critics called him a coon butcher. Sometimes he paid a high price for his sport. In 1901 he fell 58 feet to the ground. He was often bitten. Stong and coon hunting are a thing of the past in the Don Valley. With protection the picturesque coon population is multiplying.

Ernest Thompson Seton, the great Don Valley naturalist, foresaw the destruction of the coon. 'If his hollow tree and himself should meet their

A young raccoon: We are feeding him and his kind and from now on will have to put up with their tricks.

doom, it means the final conquest of the final corner of our land by the dollar and its devotees.' As I copied those lines I heard a rattling of cans— my garbage pails overturned by the coon which regularly spreads their contents about my lawns. That same evening a neighbour breathless with excitement announced the great event: five little coons had been seen a few feet from his house in the Melville ravine to the rear of Don Valley Drive.

As I lie on my veranda at night in the cottage that borders on the upper Don and listen to the ripple of the stream, I sometimes hear the shrill cry of 'Old Black Mask', the Don Valley raccoon, surveying the scene. The very forces which set out to destroy his race have been the means of his survival. From now on, we will have to put up with him and his tricks.

The Romance of the Paddle Wheel Mill

'SEASON'S GREETINGS' CARDS are frequently illustrated with drawings of old mills. A tumbling stream of water over a paddle wheel; a mill in the background usually complete the scene. These cards depict something of a romantic phase of our pioneer history. With the paddle wheel mill is associated the early growth of eastern Canada.

The paddle wheel symbolizes peace, harmony, quietude. *'Down by the Old Mill Stream', 'The Old Rustic Bridge by the mill'*; many other songs of the mill have reached us to this day from a generation of unsophisticated people who lived in simple surroundings.

The padle wheel mill was brought into the country first by the French on the lower St. Lawrence; much later by United Empire Loyalists from the American colonies. In early Southern Ontario, the paddle wheel mill was ever present; by every suitable stream flowing through a valley, one or more mills appeared. Soon, a paddle wheel was churning water and turning mill stones to grind grain into flour, or to move saws for much needed lumber.

Vestiges of pioneer mills remain in many of the old towns of Southern Ontario. A depression in the soil, a wall of river stones, pieces of rusted metal; perhaps a mill stone as well are fragments of pioneer history. In one or two instances original mills are still preserved much as they were.

After the peace of 1783, discharged soldiers (many of them from 'Butler's Rangers') and United Empire Loyalists, crossed the American border at Niagara to settle in the Niagara peninsula. They were there as a community, when John Graves Simcoe arrived to establish the first Government in that section of the Province. As it is known, the Governor selected for his capital the site on which Toronto now stands. He was quickly followed from the Niagara peninsula by settlers who saw excellent possibilities for a fresh start on the north shore of the lake.

Toronto's first mill was built late in the year 1792 on the Humber river near the lake. It was a saw mill known as the King's mill. Another saw mill was erected on the Don soon after. It was built by Timothy Skinner, a United Empire Loyalist who came to Toronto from Niagara. The Skinners, father and sons, and their 'in-law' Parshall Terry, a lieutenant in 'Butler's Rangers', played a big role in the early development of mills on the lower Don.

The first reference to this mill is to be found in Mrs. Simcoe's diary of February 3rd, 1796: *'We drove over the ice to Skinner's mill.'*

In June of 1796, Governor Simcoe issued an order to the commissary John McGill:

'You are hereby directed to give Isaiah Skinner out of His Majesty's stores, one pair of mill stones for a grist mill on the Don and a complete set of grist mill iron as encouragement for him to build a mill on the Don for accommodation for the new settlements in the neighbourhood of York.'

Isaiah Skinner was one of Timothy's sons.

This grist mill gave long, useful service. For many years it was the only grist mill on the lower Don. William Lea, founder of Leaside, relates that settlers from as far west as Hamilton brought their wheat to be ground at this mill. Boats sailed up the Don to the present Bloor street crossing, where navigation on the Don ended. There, wheat was unloaded from the boats, transferred to carts, drawn by oxen over the Don flats to the mill. The exact site is today identified by the disused Taylor paper mill on Pottery Road. People living in the backwoods simply slung a bushel of wheat over their shoulders, sometimes carrying it fifteen miles over trails through the bush to the mill, then carrying it back again as meal. One of the mill stones donated by Governor Simcoe was unearthed on the site of 'Fantasy Farm' on May 14th, 1948.

Of all pioneer mills, the Saw and Grist mills were the two most important in the early settlements. Sometimes they were operated separately; in other instances under the same roof. As population increased in the area, there followed woollen mills, carding mills, paper mills, distilleries, breweries, all depending on water for power or 'purpose'. Wm. Lyon Mackenzie the little rebel of 1837 was delighted with Shepherd's water wheel in the Don Valley near Pottery Road; it turned a stone for grinding axes.

There were many upsets in milling. The trade had its ups and downs. Settlers were awakened in the night to help fight the ice of a sudden break-up which threatened the paddle wheel. There were early morning winter calls to chop the ice away frm the frozen wheel to put it in motion again. The flood of 1878 took out every mill on the Don. Other floods less sensational side-cut mill dams leaving them high and dry. Bread was bread in those days, truly earned by the sweat of the miller's brow. Sometimes lower water level made it necessary to move a mill away from a stream entirely.

The principle of the paddle wheel mechanism was simple. A settler on the Don or elsewhere would select a suitable site for his mill. About a half-mile up the stream he built a dam. The first dams were made of logs, later of concrete. Between the mill site and the dam a trench of channel called a mill race was dug. Where the mill race joined the river by the dam, a sluice gate was placed. This permitted the shutting off of the river water from the mill race when so required. Water flowing down the mill race reached the paddle wheel of the mill by a long wooden trough called a flume. This trough carried the water from the mill race to a position directly over the paddle wheel. When the miller wished to 'turn on the water', the sluice gate up

Pottery Road as it appeared in the summer of 1900. Smoke stack marks the approximate site of Skinner's Grist mill on the Don. The apple trees on the flats are now replaced with willows. White pine trees no longer grow on the denuded slopes of Hillside Drive. The entire valley has a clean 'park like' appearance which is not true of today.

stream was opened; water raced along the channel gaining force as it went. It struck the flume at a lively speed.

The paddle wheel consisted of two huge wheels joined in a continuous manner by a number of wooden boxes or troughs. The increased weight of the water as it filled one bucket after another, caused the wheel to revolve slowly at first then more quickly. The boxes were curved slightly away from the mill to keep the splash of water from the structure.

The mechanism of a grist mill was equally simple; a shaft passed through the water wheel to the interior of the mill, where it turned a vertical wheel connected to a horizontal gear. These gears were joined to a shaft reaching from the basement to the roof of the mill. The shaft passed through a first mill stone held stationary on the ground floor of the mill. A second stone was place on the same shaft, set to revolve over the lower stone. A hopper to hold the grain was placed over the two stones. The action of a moving stone over a rigid stone produced a scissors motion which ground the wheat into flour. The stones were grooved to accentuate the grinding effect. Material used for mill gears came generally from the woods, fashioned for the most part from hard maple.

The 'Upright Frame Saw' was the first type of saw mill in use in the settlements. It was based on the principle of pioneer 'two man pit sawing', one man standing at the bottom, another at the top of the pit, sawing a log into boards between them (three hours of sawing per board). Even with water power, the 'Upright frame saw' was painfully slow to operate. Settlers referred to it as 'up today and down tomorrow'. or 'the saw which bobbed up and down'. The 'Muley saw' was the next development in saw mulls. It could be compared to a 'Cross-cut' saw held upright. Without the heavy frame of the 'Upright frame saw' it moved much faster.

The 'Muley saw' was succeeded by the 'Circular saw', which turned out most of the lumber from the original forests of Old Ontario.

Water power is still used in many grist mills in Ontario. The only remaining paddle wheel in the vicinity of Toronto is to be seen on an obscure branch of the Rouge river, north of Unionville. The paddle wheel (made of light steel) was brought from Pennsylvania. Of the original wooden paddle wheels of any of our old mills, scarcely a trace remains. In Quebec, on the north shore of the lower St. Lawrence, two or three paddle wheels are still in operation. Power is romantically supplied from falls of mountain streams.

Today, the turbine has replaced the paddle wheel. Many of the existing grist mills in Old Ontario are equipped with turbines. A turbine is described as a paddle wheel six feet in diameter placed on its side. The troughs of the paddle wheel are replaced in the turbine by inverted metal fins. The turbine is placed at the bottom of the mill. Power of amazing force is obtained through it. The turbine has been found practical in the face of a diminishing water supply, requiring much less of an elevation, consequently less water to operate it than the old paddle wheel.

In the year 1856 there were 22 mills on the west and east branches of the Don: they included 3 paper mills, 5 grist mills, 13 saw mills, 1 woollen mill. Long before 1856 the 'road' to the mills of the Don was used by settlers of the Don Valley. Timothy Skinner was given a Government order to open a road to the Don mills on March 1st, 1798.

On days when my rambles take me to the still thickly-wooded slopes below Chesterhill Road, I half expect to see an early settler come trudging through the woods, heavily laden with a sack of wheat for Skinner's Mill. If the day is drowsy and warm, a Cycada's shrill hum will conjure somewhat the notion of the whining saw of Old Timothy Skinner's Saw Mill.

Or I may place in the waters of the Don by my holdings a tiny model of a paddle wheel mill; set it up in the stream and watch the river agitate the miniature wheel, so that it turns with a lumbering gait, the water tumbling and splashing over it; the sound of moving wood and moving water emulating Philippe de Grassi's mill of 1833. A faint echo of pioneer days down the long corridor of the past.

Paper Making on the Don

AS RELATED IN THE DECEMBER 1952 ISSUE of 'The Cardinal', a grist mill was in operation on the lower Don, near the present Pottery Road as early as 1796. After the death of Parshall Terry, their ('in-law') the Skinner family became sole owners of the saw and grist mills in the lower Don. Timothy Skinner Sr. turned the mills over in due course to his son Timothy. He in turn, leased them to Samuel Sinkler, a Highland Scotsman from New Brusnwick. Skinner was killed in the battle of Chippewa, July 5th, 1814.

During the years 1814 to 1820 the mills were kept going by George Casner, a Pennsylvania Dutchman. At that time two well-known settlers, Thomas Helliwell and John Eastwood came on the Don. In 1821, Eastwood formed a partnership with Colin Skinner, a son of Isaiah Skinner, brother of Timothy Skinner Jr. They carried on the grist mill business until the year 1826 when the Government offered a bonus of (400 pounds?) to whoever would be the first to make paper in Upper Canada. The grist mill, being very much out of repair and not suited to the requirements of the country, Eastwood and Skinner determined to change it to a paper mill to get the bonus. They equipped the mill with some machinery and made paper from new stock. Wm. Lea, an early pioneer on the Don (quoted above) relates that James Crook of Flamboro West, gathered a quantity of old paper, boiled and stirred it into a pulp which he made into 'new' paper. The Government divided the bonus and gave 200 pounds to each competitor, plus duty rebates on imported machinery to Eastwood and Skinner.

The journal of the House of Assembly for Upper Canada for the period of January 8th to March 29th, 1829, records the incident somewhat differently: 'Your committee learns from Mr. Eastwood, that in consequence of the premium offered by the legislature, he and his partner Mr. Skinner commenced building a paper mill, but as Mr. James Crook had the frame of a grist mill built by the time the act was passed he immediately converted it into a paper mill and succeeded in obtaining the premium of 125 pounds.'

'Messrs. Eastwood and Skinner have persevered in this manufacture and by consuming material formerly held to be useless in the colony and producing there-from the common writing and printing papers, save within the colony large sums which used to be sent to the States.'

The report suggested that customs drawbacks be allowed on machinery imported by Eastwood and Skinner from the United States. An advertisement in the *'Colonial Advocate'* of April 17th, 1826, indicates that Skinner and Eastwood had by that time, established their paper mill:

'The subscribers having entered into a co-partnership for the purpose of converting the Don Mills into a paper mill, having most of the millwright work done, also a considerable stock of rags collected will lose no time in carrying it into operation.

'One of the partners having had many years' experience in the business both in England and the United States, they will make a good article to be sold as cheap as it can be had from the State of New York.'

'They earnestly solicit patronage of the public in saving rags, etc.'

Eastwood and Skinner's depot for rags was at the corner of King and Yonge Streets.

The Eastwood and Skinner York Paper Mill, as it was called, had its difficulties. In his *Colonial Advocate'* of February 30th, 1834, Wm. Lyon Mackenzie apologized for the bad quality of paper furnished by Eastwood and Skinner:

'Our readers may rely on it that as soon as we can remedy the evil we will not fail to do so!' In his 'Sketches of Canada' Mackenzie praised the mill in these terms: 'About three miles out of town in the bottom of a ravine watered by the river Don and bordered by beautiful and verdant flats, are situated the York paper mills, grist mill and distillery of Messrs. Eastwood and Company. I was much gratified to witness the paper manufacture in active operation and to also see the bold and pleasant scenery of the Don.'

There is some uncertainty as to the length of time the Eastwood paper making activities continued. Eastwood, according to one reference, sold the business to George Taylor in 1843. Wm. Lea sets the year at 1852. Still another reference indicates that Colin Skinner Eastwood, a son of John Eastwood, sold the Eastwood interests to the Skinner family. In 1855 Joseph Skinner is reported to have sold the paper mill property to John Taylor and Brothers, thus ending the Skinner or Eastwood families interest in the business.

It was John Eastwood who gave Todmorden (East York) its name; principally because the scenery along the Don reminded him of his English birthplace Todmorden. The Necropolis cemetery records his death as of November 17th, 1850.

In 1826 John Taylor, who had been in the country for several years, moved with his wife and family to lot eleven, concession three in the Don Valley. The original Taylor homestead still stands at the foot of Beechwood Drive. John Taylor had three sons; Thomas, George and John, who formed the paper company of John Taylor and brothers, later known as the firm of Thos. Taylor and brothers.

The next generation of Taylors to become engaged in the paper business, was formed by the three sons of George: John F., George A., and William Thos. This Wm. Taylor was the founder of the Don Valley Pressed Brick Works Co. and also the Sun Brick Co. John Hawthorne Taylor was the father of Walter Taylor of East York.

During the span of their paper making activities in the Don Valley, Taylor Brothers built three paper mills: the *'Upper Mill'*, located on the west Don, near the forks of the Don; the *'Middle Mill'*, which still stands at the foot of the present Beechwood Drive; the *'Lower Mill'*, built on, or near the site of the Eastwood mill on Pottery Road. The 'Lower Mill' was erected during the years 1845-7, as confirmed by the 'History of the County of York' in this reference: 'In 1845 John Taylor and Brothers erected their first mill on the Don River.' The 'Middle Mill' was built by the Taylors in the year 1858.

The *'Upper Mill'*, now reduced to a few ruined foundations, was built in 1846-7, largely, it is thought, through the influence of the Honourable George Brown who persuaded young John Taylor that Toronto needed another paper mill; Peter Brown, George Brown's father, came to Canada in 1842 and published a paper called *'The Banner'*. In 1844, George Brown started *'The Globe'*. The ingredients from which the paper for 'The Globe' was made in those days were rags and straw. This paper was used until pulp made of soft willow and other soft woods pushed rag newspaper off the market.

W.F.Hubbard, who died in 1935 in his 94th year, clearly remembered the winters when paper from the 'Upper Mill' used by 'The Globe' was drawn by Ox-sleigh from the mill at the forks of the Don, up the steep hill leading out of the valley to Don Mills Road and finally over the Queen Street bridge to the printing plant of 'The Globe.'

This interesting reference to the 'Upper Mill' appears in *'Canada, Past, Present and Future'* published in 1851:

'After re-ascending the bank it is about two and a half miles to Taylor's Paper mill. There is also a saw mill and the river here has a fall of 23 feet. The damming of the river at this spot floods about 30 acres of land.'

This pond is shown on Tremaines map of the area.

'Illustrated Toronto' of 1877, related that the mills
"... supply a very large portion of the printing paper now used for the daily and weekly newspapers of this city (Toronto) and throughout the Dominion.' 'There is also manufactured at the mills coloured paper, poster bills, book, manilla, roll, expressing, tea and common paper bags. Hundred of tons of rags, straw, esparto grass, ropes, canvas are used in the manufacture of this useful economy.'
A hundred hands were employed. The paper output was four tons every twelve hours.

There is little mention of the activities of the 'Lower Mill'. In its heyday it was an important factor in the Taylor enterprises. Successive fires closed it down entirely.

The 'Middle Mill' was turbine operated. A mill race leading from a concrete dam which stood in the Don near the present Leaside bridge supplied water for the turbine. All during its long life the 'Middle Mill' continued to function as a paper mill. In 1927 it was operated by the Don

In 1927 the 'Middle Mill' was operated by Don Valley Paper Company. It became a unit of Howard Smith Paper Mills Limited in 1939.
Snapshot of the 'Lower Mill' on Pottery Road as it stands today; John Eastwood's house (see Sketch) stood across the road from the mill.

Valley Paper Co. It became a unit of Howard Smith Paper Mills (its present owners) in 1939. Pulp is no longer made on the premises. It is brought in by rail in bundles, similar in appearance to folded blankets. From this pulp is manufactured cover stock in various colors for catalogues. Blotting paper is a major item.

Today, a less abundant Don moves languidly past the sites of the three mills: of the 'Upper Mill' there remains scarcely a trace. Until 1942, the walls were intact. The huge pine rafters were still in place. The mill then could easily have been preserved as an historical site. During the second world war, the timbers were taken from it by a saw mill owner who ruined the walls during the demolition. The foundations are plainly visible on the west Don near the forks of the Don, a few rods from th C.N.R. line.

The 'Middle Mill' still serves the original purpose for which it was built. It is to be regarded as an historical Don Valley landmark. Of the 'Lower Mill', only a portion of the original building remains. Thirty years ago trout were fished from its 'race', the brick work of which is still visible from Pottery Road. Below the rubble near the 'Upper Mill', may yet be found the original foundations of the Skinner grist mill and its successor the Eastwood paper mill.

56

The dams built to supply water in quantity for each of the mills have either been washed out or blown up. Two of these dams were destroyed as a menace to juvenile bathers in the Don.

The story of paper on the Don is a story one might say of 'rags to riches'; from the rags used in Eastwood's crude mill to the great enterprises of today. While little paper mills of yesteryear would be considered quaint in the ranks of the giants of present-day industry, they should be remembered as a tribute to the courage of those men who launched a new industry in a new country.

Spring 1953

Sugar Loaf Hill–Rosedale Ravine

THE SUGAR LOAF HILL stands within a stone's throw of the north rampart of the Prince Edward Viaduct. 'Toronto of Old' describes it as a singular isolated mound. Other early Toronto writings refer to it as: 'the most picturesque spot near Toronto'; 'a most singular conical hill—an immense Indian tumulus for the dead.'

In the Don river, at the base of Sugar Loaf Hill a generation ago, was a swimming hole known as 'Sandy Point'. Here the river moved in a swift current over treacherous sands, scene of repeated drownings. The exact location of 'Sandy Point' was in the shadow thrown eastward over the Don by Sugar Loaf Hill.

Immediately below 'Sandy Point' was the 'Ford', on a line with the concession road (Bloor Street) where the earliest traffic crossed over to the Danforth avenue side of the valley. The 'Ford' was described as 'a convenient means of communication between Chester and Yorkville.'

During the French regime the 'Ford' was on a trail leading to Montreal. It was used by Indians, fur traders, and adventurers of the woods. Early in the nineteenth century, the 'Ford' and the Sugar Loaf Hill marked the end of navigation on the Don for small lake vessels which brought wheat to be ground in the grist mill a half-mile up the valley from the 'Ford'.

On October 18th, 1918, the Bloor Street viaduct was opened to traffic. Construction of the bridge was started on January 7th, 1915. With the advent of the viaduct, Sugar Loaf Hill could no longer be seen, 'set down in the midst of the valley, seated among fields and woods.'

The visitor who glanced down from the ramp of the viaduct, sees the top of the hill almost level with the floor of the bridge. The C.N.R. line flanks the hill on the east. North-westwards, a panorama of woodland (Old Drum-

The Don Valley at Bloor Street crossing. January 1915. Photo shows the beginning of the construction of Bloor Street viaduct. Note, Sugar Loaf Hill with Rosedale ravine extreme right background.

snab), becomes in summer a vista of undulating waves of billowy leafage, extending towards Rosedale ravine. The slopes are heavily wooded. In winter, one sees the Rosedale brook meandering through the ravine of that name, emptying into the Don. Rosedale ravine got its name from the thousands of wild roses which once carpeted its slopes. The Rosedale brook enters the Don valley through the meadows of Captain George Playter's one-time Crown grant.

Across the Don from the Rosedale ravine stood Helliwell's bush. Even in 1880, it was the haunt of wild pigeons, partridges and small animals. The common fruits of the woodland grew there. 'Shinnies' and clothes props were cut in Helliwell's bush by the hundreds. The fine old Beech trees and other species of the original forest have long since disappeared. Hop gardens covered the flats of the valley near the bush. The crop was used in Helliwell's brewery.

'Sandy Point' swimming hole and Helliwell's bush were reached by boys from Yorkville, via 'stumpy field', on the south side of South Drive, east of Sherbourne street. The field was noted for its Beech nuts and wild Strawberries.

In the Don valley, north of the viaduct, stood Jimmy Young's rendering 'establishment': old fat was here prepared for use in soap making. Young and sons, (the official name of the firm) also operated a horse abattoir.

Don Kindling company was a companion industry of Young's. It had the distinction of being the last saw mill in operation in the Don valley. In the early days a brick works was located on the east side of the valley, where the viaduct now spans it.

Spring 1953

The Last of Old Jim's Orchard

UNTIL HIS DYING DAY 'Old Jim' remembered the apple seeds. The Governor had received a small bagful of them from Samuel Ogden of New York, distributing them promptly among the early settlers around Toronto. 'Old Jim' had pocketed his supply on that Saturday afternoon, returning to his homestead over the trails through the valley; tall pines everywhere, a clearing here and there. Near the grist mill he stopped to count the seeds, the water from the river churning pleasantly over the huge creaking paddle wheel: one hundred in all. His wife had scoffed a little over his enthusiasm: *'Apple trees in a country of bush and stumps, of bears, wolves and what not.'* A potato that would grow close to a burned stump then, was worth a whole bushel of apples which could only be had ten years hence when there would be no stumps.

'Old Jim' was no fool. There was something of the nursery man in him. He put the seeds in moist sand for a few weeks, set them outside in a row, where he could look after them properly. They sprouted, produced shoots and that season grew a foot or so. Might have been the first nursery in these parts for all 'Old Jim' knew.

He waited a few years until the apple seedlings had grown to four or five feet, with a good framework on which to hang someday a heavy crop; when the clearing where he planned to transplant them would be free of stumps. He remembered that second Saturday quite as well as the first—the day he transplanted all of the hundred seedlings, with great caution, placing carefully the virgin roots in the virgin soil and poking into a suggestion of gravel which told him instinctively that apples would do ever-so-well with that drainage.

'Old Jim' had to wait a little for the first crop. By then, the trail across the valley wasn't as narrow as it used to be. He could see beyond his own fields. The forest was disappearing. He had neighbours, people who told him that they had never tasted apples such as his—great 'whoppers', good for eating, cooking and storing, against the days when an iron cold froze the earth of the orchard to iron, it seemed. And the seed saved was passed on to 'Old Jim's' sons and daughters homesteading fifty miles north of the lake.

'Old Jim's' orchard grew to where it could fend for itself; the trunks of the trees strong enough for cattle to lean against and the bark too tough for even a famished rodent to gnaw at. By then, 'Old Jim' counted his harvest by the barrelful; the fruit always good, no disease ever affecting it.

But, an apple tree has a tenaciously long life and when 'Old Jim's' had petered out, the orchard it seemed was virile enough for another generation or two of the old man's family. By then it was an orchard in a countryside, along with other orchards and the first dwellings of a new town: Leaside they called it with a tiny station for the new railway tracks that skirted 'Old Jim's' orchard.

For forty years, perhaps a few more, the orchard was caught in a backwash; on land that someoen owned without using. The fruit had dwindled in size; sucker growth had thickened along the branches. Only the robins and the urchins visited the trees. Then one day, it happened. Men came with horses and plows and other equipment and in almost a day 'Old Jim's' orchard of a century collapsed. All of the trees had been cut, save one; the old knarled 'Spy' with the deep hole, for the possession of which Starlings—a new bird in the country—fought each Spring—just a stone's throw from the old railway station.

For years, the venerable tree could well have inherited all the decapitated life of the other roots, as though anchored forever; always the same in a changing world. A world of smoke stacks, road machinery, tractors, traffic, giant locomotives which shrieked as they thundered past the tree, with a mile of box cars trailing on behind—things that 'Old Jim' had never dreamed of.

Shades of the pioneers! The old apple tree would have survived this new generation too, keeping tryst with its past, had it not been for the old station. An old apple tree could grow on unnoticed, but with a small station in a growing community things are different: passengers needed more room and they got it.

Today, there stands a new station replacing the old one, and in the sleek parking lot adjoining it, away down under the macadam, lie entombed the roots of *the last of Old Jim's orchard*.

'Castle Frank'

SEEN FROM THE SOUTH SIDE RAMP of the Prince Edward Viaduct directly above the C.N.R. tracks, one observes, flanking these tracks on the west, a series of indented hills, adjoining a plateau. On this plateau a hundred feet above the Don stood, in 1796, *Governor and Mrs. Simcoe's 'Castle Frank'*.

The Simcoes, newly arrived at the site of Toronto and desirous of providing themselves with a country retreat, selected as the most picturesque place for it, the plateau on the bluff by the Don. Mrs. Simcoe describes her first journey to this place, as a climb, up an exceedingly steep hill, then along a series of sugar-loaf hills, from whence she could look down upon the tops of the large trees in which eagles had built their nests. *'The Governor talks of placing a canvas house on this point for a summer residence,'* she wrote, and again, on October 29th, 1793: *'The Governor having determined to take a lot of 200 acres upon the river Don for Francis and as the law obliges persons having lots of land to build a house upon them within a year, we went today to fix upon the spot for building a house.'*

By the Spring of 1794 'Castle Frank' was in use. Its style was referred to as that of a Grecian temple. Its large main room had a fireplace. Behind the fireplace stood another room the dimensions of the first. Four shuttered windows adorned both of the side walls of the building. The castle was built entirely of White Pine. Four Pine logs supported the projecting veranda roof.

The windows which lighted the underground room were cut through the side of the hill; it was a place to which the Simcoes could retire in very hot weather: 'Castle Frank' was eighty feet long, 40 feet wide and 20 feet to the eaves.

'Castle Frank' became the centre of social activity for the garrison stationed at Toronto and the focal point of interest for the Simcoes during their stay in York. Mrs. Simcoe mentioned it frequently in her diary. In February 1796 she told of driving over the ice to 'Castle Frank' and dining there with a party of ladies from the garrison.

In summer, 'Castle Frank' could be reached by boat from the fort or by following a trail along the present Yonge Street and easterly to the Don, via Pine glades, free of underbrush ("pleasant shady Pine plains covered with sweet-scented ferns"). The favourite route was by water from the fort, along to the Bay and up the Don.

One of Mrs. Simcoe's choice diary entries, dated July 1st, 1796, records the visit of a large party from the garrison to 'Castle Frank' for dinner. A boat with music (a band) accompanied them. After dinner she could hear the music until the boats had 'passed the town'. *It sounded delightful* she said—military music echoing along the Pine-clad wilderness of the Toronto of 1796.

No prettier spot could have been selected for the Governor's summer home than the site of 'Castle Frank'. The plateau on the bluff on the Don was covered with White Pine. From the lofty view, the bosky valley retreated northward. To the south, a vista of wooded slopes culminated in the straight, blue horizon line of the distant lake. The Pines were of huge girth. After the return of the Simcoes to England, Commissary McGill gave strict orders that the trees were not to be cut down. The lower Don valley was a boundless wilderness then compared with today. On the other side of the plateau was the ravine of 'Castle Frank' and the brook of that name.

Now all is changed. The stumps of the virgin White Pine have long since rotted awayl a few distant relatives of a later generation of the species still remain. White Oak trees have replaced the Pine. A road travels through the ravine, through which the brook of 'Castle Frank' still flows, but through a bricked-over channel. Southerly from the plateau stretches Riverdale Park. To the north the massive arches of Prince Edward Viaduct gird figuratively to the loins of the valley.

Under 'Castle Frank's' gay roof, appeared historical figures: the Indian chief, Captain Joseph Brant; Captain Walter Butler of Butler's Rangers, and others.

Map 754 made prior to the erection of 'Castle Frank' shows exactly the geographical approaches to the place: the path leading from the west bank of the Don from a point where 'Castle Frank' brook emptied into the Don; the path skirting the side of the Hog's Back' hill to the plateau on which stood the Chateau; a third path leading directly from 'York'. The worn lines of these bridle and foot paths made by Governor Simcoe and parties are still discernible in places along the side of the 'Hog's Back' and can be followed to the ridge above, They lie on the 'Castle Frank' ravine side of the hill.

Mrs. Simcoe left 'Castle Frank' on July 21, 1798; a sad hour and one which found her so out of spirits that she cried most of the day. 'Castle Frank' often called the 'park' was used by members of the administration and of the garrison. The Hon. Peter Russell, and the Chief Justice, Mr. Elmsley, resided there "and has requested (Elmsley) permission to occupy 'Castle Frank', which request I have complied with on the condition that none of the trees on the high ground are to be cut down.' And again on September 27, 1797, a letter from McGill to Simcoe: 'The Chief Justice gave occasional dinners there during the sitting of Parliament. I have permitted Mr. Russell's relative, Captain Dennison, to reside at 'Castle Frank' on the condition of his not cutting down a tree or suffering a road through the enclosure.' On June 8th, 1798: 'Pray what are the arrangements you (Governor Simcoe)

Close-up sketch of 'Castle Frank' brook, also called the 'Brewers Creek' and 'Severn's Creek'. Sketch shows the brewery of Jos.Bloor in the ravine midway between Sherbourne Street and Huntley bridge. The Sherbourne Street blockhouse (see sketch) stood at the head of Sherbourne Street on an exact line with Bloor Street. It was part of a system of defense to protect the city from the north during the rebellion of 1837. Sketches from *Robertson's Landmarks*.

wish to have made in regard to 'Castle Frank'. The Chief Justice has a great partiality for the situation.' It would seem from these and other letters of the time, that 'Castle Frank' filled on several occasions a breach in the housing shortage of early York or Toronto.

There is a further record of 'Castle Frank' on July 17, 1803: Colonel Talbot wrote to General Simcoe telling him of the sorry fate which was slowly overtaking 'that pretty spot on the Don': *'I paid a visit to 'Castle Frank' which I am sorry to add is uninhabited and going to ruin. Some rascals had a few days before I saw it, broken off the window shutters and gone down the chimney in order to carry away the bar iron that supported it.'*

'Castle Frank' survived the war of 1812, despite the importance which the American invaders of 1813 placed on it. It was ransacked during a search for the papers and gold of the administration of York, both of which were thought by the invading force to be hidden somewhere along the Don. In 1829 the building, in utter disuse, was burnt to the ground accidentally by persons it is thought, who used the place while salmon fishing in the Don.

The name 'Castle Frank' could have been selected from several sources: Governor Simcoe may have had his son Francis in mind, 'Frank' for Francis; or it may have come from Castel-Franc in the southwest of France, a place with which the Governor was familiar.

Throughout the years the name 'Castle Frank' has been handed down from generation to generation of Toronto schoolboys. Few, indeed, do not know of the lofty plateau along which gay parties long, long ago rode to the rustic summer home of the Simcoes.

The site of 'Castle Frank' was marked at one time with a commemorative stone, of which there is no evidence today. The upper half of a large boulder protrudes from the plateau a short distance south of the site of 'Castle Frank'. By rubbing charcoal over the face of this boulder, I was able to discern the figures 1796 and to the left of this date, the letters A.H.M.V. and Y.O.C.U.

'Castle Frank' brook gained two other names throughout the years. The 'Brewer's Creek' and 'Severn's Creek'. The creek was known throughout the community for its association with the Don Vale Tavern and Fox's Inn, both of which stood on the same site on the west bank of the Don near the present Winchester Street bridge.

The creek earned these pseudonymns from the breweries still built along it; namely the Yorkville Brewery and the Bloor Brewery. John Severn and his son George operated the Yorkville brewery during the period of 1832 to 1899. This brewery stood on the west side of Yonge Street north of Davenport Road.

The brewery of Joseph Bloor, in operation in 1833, was situated in 'Castle Frank' ravine, midway between Sherbourne Street and Huntley bridge. This brewery stood in the ravine on the south bank of the creek a few yards from the Bloor Street of today. The creek rose north of St. Clair Avenue, folowed the ravine across Yonge Street at Tannery Hollow to empty in the Don by Winchester Street. It was eventually bricked-over and turned into a sewer.

Bloor's mill-pond adjoined the brewery. It was a glorious bathing place for the boys of that time: a fine skating rink for them in winter. At the head of Sherbourne Street on the exact line of Bloor Street, stood a military blockhouse, a defence unit designed to protect the city from the north during the rebellion of 1837. It was twenty-five feet square and built of hewn Pine logs and was garrisoned by fifty men. An island stood in the Don, almost at the mouth of 'Castle Frank' brook. In the stream at the northern end of this point, wild rice grew in abundance. In the Fall large numbers of water fowl gathered there. Remains of Indian encampments, tusks of bears, fragments of pottery have been found close by.

The long, narrow 'camel back' type of ridge distinguishes the hills in the valley between the Winchester bridge and the viaduct. Several of these Hog's Backs, as they are called, are to be seen on both sides of the Don River below Bloor Street.

Fall 1953

Early Exploration and Settlement
of the Lower Don Valley

IN SEPTEMBER OF 1615, ETIENNE BRULE CAME TO THE MOUTH OF THE HUMBER RIVER. He was the first white man to see Lake Ontario. In 1669, the Sulpicians, an order of French priests, explored the entire contour of Lake Ontario. Neither Brule or the Sulpicians made any reference to the Don. In 1688, Father Pierre Raffeix, a Jesuit priest, explored the Don River and included it on his map of the north shore of Lake Ontario. Father Raffeix is, therefore, the first known man to have left any record of the Don river.

A long gap in the years must be filled with surmise as to further exploration along the Don. Fort Rouille or Fort Toronto stood, during the period of 1750-1759, near the lake shore on the Exhibition grounds of today.. During those years, we may be sure that French soldiers of the garrison and French sailors from visiting craft, found their way up the sylvan valley of the Don to enjoy many an hour fishing, hunting and exploring in the unbroken wilderness. Other Frenchmen of whom we know nothing, undoubtedly ascended the valley on their way to the north.

A record of the presence of a white man near the Don, is gleaned from the diary of Captain Walter Butler of Butler's Rangers. He journeyed past the river on the 16th of March 1779. He limits his remarks to mention of a *'camping place where the high lands (Scarboro Bluffs) began.'*

In 1788, the surveyor Aitkin made a map which included the Don with this reference: 'navigable for a boat for two or three miles.'

In 1789, Hypolite La Force along with Kotte and Peachy surveyed the north shore of Lake Ontario. La Force's reference to the Don is unmistakable: *'went into the swamp at the bottom of the bay and into a small river running N.N.W. for near two miles. It is deep and then winding. There is good timber and Pine on its banks. On the East side we found a small cabin not finished, marked George Cocker, 18th of June 1789, but no land cleared near it.'* La Force was among the last to defend the French flag in Canada and among the first to take up the cause of the British.

On May 2, 1793, Governor Simcoe, who had been at Newark (Niagara) since July 26, 1792, made a first visit to study the present site of Toronto as a possible location for the capital of Upper Canada. Referring to this visit, an old document relates: *'They found only one English family, that of Wm.Peake and three Indian wigwams east of the Don.'*

In September 1793, Governor Simcoe set out with a party to explore the possibilities of a communicating route between Toronto and Lake Huron. In that year, war with the American colonies seemed imminent, and Toronto a most strategic spot in the possible conflict. The Chevalier de Rochblave had suggested to Simcoe that warships on Lake Ontario and Lake Huron could be manned by the same crews transported overland in any emergency providing a suitable route could be found. After an absence of two weeks Simcoe 'discovered a trail from the Holland Landing to the mouth of the Don which answered all expectations.' *Thus Yonge Street was born.*

The return journey took Simcoe's party along several branches of the Don. On September 13th, the soldiers had breakfast near the source of the German creek and almost on the site of Elgin Mills. The party then followed the German Creek for a distance, struck southwards between it and the line of Yonge Street and came on the east branch of the Don about two miles below Thornhill, where they encamped. On the 14th they again camped, this time on the west branch of the Don about a mile and a half below York Mills.

Surveyor Jones in his notes of the Yonge Street survey made in 1794, mentions 'Coon's road.' John Coon, a sergeant in Butler's Rangers, was probably the first settler on the Don, following the squatter mentioned by La Force. On September 11th, 1793, Mrs. Simcoe and party 'rowed six miles up the Don to Coon's who has a farm under a hill covered with Pine.' *'I landed to see the shingles made,'* she said, *'which is done by splitting large blocks of pine in equal divisions.'*

Coon's hill is now cut through by the C.P.R. high level bridge. The Don Valley Brick works is on the site of his farm. The scene now is much different from that Summer day in 1796 when Mrs. Simcoe 'walked through the meadows towards Coon's farm and saw millions of yellow and black butterflies dancing and flying about.'

In the Spring of 1794, a party of German and Pennsylvania Dutch settlers, under the leadership of William Berczy, made their way up the east Don to a branch stream later known as the German Creek. They established a settlement and built mills on this creek east of Thornhill.

When Governor and Mrs. Simcoe took up quarters in Toronto, they were followed by a number of settlers, some from the Niagara Peninsula, others from England. Among the former were the Skinners and Playters. The latter group included John Scadding of Devon origin and manager of Wolford, the Simcoe estate in England. He arrived in Canada shortly after the Simcoes and followed them to York, presumably in the Fall of 1793. He drew as a grant, Lot 15 with broken front, extending from the water's edge of the bay, to the first concession line, now Danforth Avenue.

John Scadding returned to England, with the Simcoes, in 1796. He came out to Canada again in April of 1818, and took up settlement once more on lot 15. The Scadding cabin which stands in Exhibition park today, was

The Scadding cabin pictured in this old print was removed from the Don at Queen Street to Exhibition Park in 1879. The cabin was built in 1794 by William Smith for John Scadding.

removed there in 1879. It stood originally on the Don near Queen Street. It was built by William Smith in 1794.

William Smith was with Simcoe on his first visit to Toronto. Smith planned many of the public buildings of the embryo city and drew the plans for 'Castle Frank'. He purchased the lower part of Lot 15 from John Scadding who moved to another section of his lot and erected a permanent dwelling on the site of the present Don Jail. Here John Scadding practised gardening and farming on a scale previously unknown in 'Upper Canada'.

In a veritable wilderness, he planted wheat, rye, barley, oats and corn, and an orchard containing a variety of apples and other fruit, interestingly enough the Peach and Siberian Crab. Near his log house he cultivated melons of several varieties and grew many vegetables, including Asparagas and Celery. It is said that he introduced the PiePlant (Rhubarb) to the Don Valley. His flower garden included the common flowers of England and several kind of Rose bushes.

The flats beyond the house became meadows in which sheep and cattle grazed. Mr. Scadding attempted to improve the marsh lands adjoining the river by cutting channels through them. 'The lofty and steep hillsides along the stream presented very picturesque scenery.' John Scadding died on March 1st, 1824. His son, Dr. Henry Scadding, became the foremost historian of the Don. He left in several volumes, a wealth of detail on the early settlement of the Don.

There is much to remind us of the name Playter. It is a familiar one to persons living in the Danforth-Broadview area. On September 4, 1793, Colonel George Playter acquired land on the Don. Born in England, he emigrated from that country to Philadelphia. After the American Revolution, Colonel George and his son James moved to Kingston, 'Upper Canada'. They then came to the town of York. The Department of Legislative Reference, City Hall Baltimore, Maryland, records the fact that George Playter was Governor of Maryland in the year 1791.

There are several reference to the Playter's in Mrs. Simcoe's diary:

JUNE 1, 1795: *'I drank tea at Playter's.'*

JULY 4, 1796: *'I walked to Skinner's mill through the Meadows. Playter was haymaking.'*

JULY 6, 1796: *'I passed Playter's picturesque bridge over the Don. It is a Butternut tree, fallen across the river.'*

This tree spanned the Don on the site of the present Winchester Street bridge. (see map, page 7, 'Cardinal', June 1953 issue).

Colonel George's house stood immediately north of 'Castle Frank', on the site of the A.E.Kemp residence, No. 2 Castle Frank Crescent. During the construction of this residence in 1902, workmen uncovered the stone foundations of George Playter's residence of 1795.

Captain John Playter resided on the east side of the valley, approximately near the angle of Cambridge and Danforth Avenues.

The first settlers on the Don were soon followed by many others. Their names appear in the Land books, tersely associated with the parcelling-off of the valley into 200 acre grants.

The days of the early settlement of the Don were among the most picturesque in Toronto's history. The 'long beach' or peninsula of which Toronto Island was once a part, was resorted to by the Indians when indisposed. It was also used by members of the garrison for horse-back riding from the mouth of the Don to the heights of Scarboro. Toronto Marsh and Ashbridge's Bay were a 'tangled wilderness'; a wonderful bird paradise, once the home of many of the rare birds of Ontario.

Those were the days, when crude traffic bridges were thrown across the Don, the first of which was the Scadding bridge erected at the junction of King and Queen Streets.

Every spring of water in those days was considered by the settlers as a potential site for a 'still'. Potash factories stood close to the banks of the lower Don. The first mills began to rip into planks the magnificent White Pine trees for which the Don Valley was once famous. Distillers and brewers plied their trade.

Thirty pound Salmon were taken then from the Don. Every brook was 'Trout Creek'. Passenger Pigeons darkened the skies in their flights over the valley. Most of the Hemlocks were ruined, when stripped of their bark for use in the tanneries. In those days ice remained on Toronto bay until May.

Fall 1953

Artists, Writers, Poets, Hikers of the Don

THE DON VALLEY HAS HELD A FASCINATION for people who love the beautiful in nature, from the time the valley in all its primeval grandeur was first seen by the first person able to appreciate its beauty. Today, men and women in growing numbers love the valley for its trees, birds, scenery, wild flowers and tranquillity. Every generation of Toronto citizens has produced a new race of adherents to the Don Valley.

Mrs. Simcoe heads chronologically the list of artists, hikers and ramblers of the Don. Her diary and sketches constitute the only full record of the Don Valley of the later eighteenth century. Through Mrs. Simcoe the history of the beginning of settlement on the Don has been narrated.

Dr. Henry Scadding, the son of John Scadding, who came to Canada with the Simcoes, earned his title 'Yeoman of the Don.' His 'Toronto of Old', the best known of his works, deals extensively with the Don, but there are other Scadding writings, some published, some in manuscript form, which record the history of the Simcoes and those who followed them. To John Scadding's pen, fell the task of retaining recollections of Toronto, as it emerged from the bush.

PAUL KANE was Toronto's first artist. His parents settled in Toronto in 1808. As a lad he spent much of his time sketching and rambling through the valley, often in the company of the Mississauga Indians whose encampment lay on the flats at the mouth of the Don. *'I have been accustomed to see,'* he writes, *'hundreds of Indians about my native village of 'Little York''*.

ANNA BROWNELL JAMESON, the wife of a 'Little York' official, penned a detailed description of the Toronto of 1837, and particularly of the lake front and the wild life sanctuary created by the Toronto marsh. About the same time, Wm.Lyon Mackenzie (the little rebel) made himself familiar with the Don Valley, where many of his pre-rebellion partisans lived. He left us descriptions of the 'early mills near the beautiful and verdant flats.'

PHILIPPE DE GRASSI was virtually unknown, until it fell to my good fortune to recover his diary and to piece together the story of this pioneer of the

Forks of the Don. He left us an account of early settlement in that area. We now know that it was de Grassi's daughter 'Cornelia', who saved Toronto from the Mackenzie forces in 1837.

About 1870, ERNEST THOMPSON SETON began his rambles up the Don, which through his writings became world famous. In the setting of an unspoiled valley, he played Indian and later wrote 'Two Little Savages', based on his adventures in the valley: also 'Wild Animals I Have Known' and other books now sold the world over.

It has been said that Seton was tutored in his knowledge of the valley by Dr. W.A.Brodie, a parliament street dentist. Seton was accompanied in some of his rambles by Macpherson Ross of the Toronto nursery firm of that name. Ross wrote and sketched for the 'Toronto Telegram'.

In 1885 JOHN ROSS ROBERTSON published his incomparable six volumes, 'Robertson's Landmarks of Toronto'. The volumes contain information which 'Telegram' reporters of the time secured from the descendants of pioneers of the valley. The late Owen Staples did much of the illustrating for the 'Landmarks'.

OWEN STAPLES was an inveterate rambler and spent much of his time painting and writing in the valley. He produced 'scenery on canvas' in every season. Some of his paintings of early Toronto are to be seen in the corridors of Toronto City Hall. His 'American Invasion of York' gives an artist's conception of the Don Valley of 1814. Mr. Staples wrote and sketched extensively on Don valley subjects for 'The Telegram'. In 1885 FRED BRIGDEN took over the Don Valley as his own particular hobby. Mr. Brigden is probably the only man who has walked both the East and West Don valleys in their full length, sketching all the way. He has produced dozens of paintings of the Don in all seasons. T.V.MARTIN and MANLY MACDONALD, both artists of note, have painted in the valley. C.W.JEFFERYS, the famous historical illustrator, painted a series of water color scenes of the lower Don. A.P.Coleman wrote extensively on Don vallaey geology.

Mention is made of contemporary bird columnists, ANNE MARRILL, JIM BAILLIE, HUGH HALLIDAY, who have made frequent mention of the valley in their weekly columns. The dean of all Don Valley newspaper columnists was W.F.(Billy)MacLean, owner of the 'Toronto World'. In the early 1900's he wrote abundantly on the Don. Feature stories of the 'World's' Sunday Supplement were frequently based on the colorful adventures of the 'Don Valley Nature Study Club', of which he was the founder. MacLean owned several hundreds of acres on the Don, including the present Donlands Farm and Milne's Hollow.

The hikers of the Don are without number. Who will ever know all the people who walked up the Don from childhood to old age; those who wrote stories, others who told them; old men's tales which died with them.

STUART L. THOMPSON, nephew of Ernest Thompson Seton and undoubtedly the best all round naturalist to ever visit the valley, started his rambles in May of 1900 and he is still rambling. Stuart has won wide recognition as an imitator of bird songs.

70

FRANK SMITH, who carves birds in wood, played along the Don at the turn of the century. The McArthurs (beemen) were established in the valley sixty years ago. The poetry of I.M.MCARTHUR is an equisite treasure from the soul of a man to whom the valley was always home. BERT OLSEN, the movie photographer of the valley, spends his leisure time filming in colour its beauties in all seasons. I have rambled along the Don, *'times without number'* with no claim to distinction other than a poetic sense of the valley's beauty and an enthusiasm for gathering the fragments of its history.

MISS EDNA BREITHAUPT of Wakunda Art Centre and ROY CADWELL conceived the idea of a Don Valley School of Art. The club's chalet stands today on Don Mills Road near the forks of the Don. Hundreds of artists of the Don have already associated themselves with it, spreading through their work the beauty of the valley far and wide: Bill Boston, Margaretta Stevens, Mrs. Mary Roche, Leslie Radcliffe, Dorothy Dennison, and others, have done their large share in the carrying on of this work.

The Don Valley has played host, and still plays host, to many of the outstanding botanists and writers of this day. In a half-mile walk, one may meet a man who has written a book on birds, or who has collected all of the local species of plants.

Winter 1953

The Forks of the Don

THE NAME, FORKS OF THE DON, *applies to the meeting place of the three main branches of the Don* which occurs on Lot 6, concession 3, East York. These stream are: the East Branch of the Don; the West Branch of the Don; and a smaller stream known as Silver Creek, Taylor Creek and Scarboro Creek.

In the vicinity of the forks, four great ravines meet. Two of these ravines are formed by the east valley, above and below the forks; the other two ravines consist of the west valley of the Don and the ravine known as Taylor's bush.

The immediate vicinity of the forks contains wide meadowlands, encompassed by lofty valley walls covered with many kinds of deciduous trees, interspersed with White Pine, Cedar and Hemlock.

Near the centre of the forks of the Don stands a tomb-like hill, flat at the top, precipitous on the east and north sides, where it flanks Don Mills Road and Silver Creek, sloping gently to the south towards the ravine of Taylor's Bush.

This hill was known as Greenlands, or Greenlands Mount, because of the dense Cedar and Hemlock which once covered it. In the shelter of this evergreen foliage, ice clung to the steep northern slope generations ago, long into Summer. Today Greenslades is still green, but much less so than in the pioneer days of the country. Greenlands was also called Tumper's Hill; a settler of that name lived in a cabin on the flat top of the mount.

A climb to the lofty crest of the mount rewards one with a dominating view of the entire forks of the Don. The east Don is seen as it follows a straight course to its meeting palce with Silver Creek, almost at the base of Greenlands. These two streams, united, journey on to meet a few hundred feet further west, the west branch of the Don, just beyond the 'White bridge'.

Don Mills road follows its asphalt course out of the valley, northwards, via the steep long grade of de Grassi's Hill. Also to be seen are wide stretches of the east valley and the entrance to the west valley. A small vehicle bridge spans the west Don near the ruins of the Taylor 'Upper' paper mill. From this bridge commences a picturesque climb out of the valley to Thorncliffe. It is a tree-bordered county lane, alive in Summer with bird song and adorned with the shrubbery and the flowers of the country-side.

'The neighbourhood of the forks, where there is a small village, abounds in romantic scenery. The wildness and beauty of the ravines, glens and stretches of woodland present attractions for the lover of nature not readily surpassed in this part of Canada.'

Another quotation from an early writing, describes the forks as *'the prettiest bit of landscape in the neighbourhood.'* At the turn of the century, it was a bustling little community with its paper mill, saw mill, orchards of prize apple trees, neat little country homes surrounded with picket fences; also the unhurried buggy and hay-rig traffic of dusty Don Mills Road. Crowning this scene was the farm of 'King Bob' Davies, where deer and buffalo were once kept in enclosures. The stately southern-style mansion with its tall Spruce trees was then the home of a family which owned one of the finest farms in Ontario. Prize herds of cattle roamed the verdant flats of the west valley of the Don. In pioneer records the forks of the Don was known as the boatbildery. *'I drew as my grant parts of lots 6 and 7, 200 acres on the Don, of what was then known as the boat bildery.'* This pioneer record was dated 1833. We can assume that small craft were once built on the Don near the forks.

D.W.SMITH, the Surveyor General of Governor Simcoe's time, at least entertained the thought of erecting a saw mill and grist mill on the Don on Lot 6 by the present Todmorden Park.

Closely associated with the Forks of the Don is the story of the North-West Company formed in the winter of 1783-4 by Jospeh Frobisher and Simon McTavish. With the opening of Yonge Street, the men of the North-West Company began to journey along the north shore of Lake Ontario to

York (Toronto) in preference to the former trade route to Lake Huron via the Ottawa River or the circuitous route of Lake Erie. Accordingly, each Spring for several years following the arrival of Governor Simcoe at York, the bateaux of the North-West Company men reached York. They stopped at the Peninsula, portaged from there to the bay, ascended the Don river to the forks, then followed its west branch to Yonge Street. At the place later known as Hogg's Hollow, the boats were lashed to wheels and pulled up the newly-made road to the Holland River. The journey then continued by water to the Great Lakes.

Today the story of the North-West Company is history and the west Don a brook; a stream for a boy's toy boat. The deeper water which held the bateaux of the boatmen is gone and with it the memory of the Scotch and French voyageurs who once plied a difficult trade.

PHILLIPE DE GRASSI was born on the 15th day of May 1793, on the opposite side of the Tiber immediately in front of the Castle of Saint Angelo and the Vatican in Rome. His father, Alfio Mariano Grassi was a celebrated lawyer. His mother, Anna Elizabetha Brumaritz, was daughter of Baron Joannie Brumaritz of Vienna, Austria.

Phillipe de Grassi was educated in France and saw military service in Spain with the French army. He was taken prisoner and sent to England. He continued his military career and saw service with the British army in the West Indies. He returned to England. In that country he taught languages for sixteen years and made many influential friends.

For reasons of health he was advised to emigrate to Canada. He embarked at Southampton towards the end of July 1831, along with his wife and eight children, on the 'Proesis.' The de Grassi's arrived at Toronto, then little York, on September 19, 1831.

De Grassi drew a grant of 200 acres on the Don in the area described as the 'Boatbildery'. He 'at once' took possession of this estate, getting it chopped up and cleared and a house put up.

During the winter Captain de Grassi and his eldest son 'used to go' to and from the property to inspect operations. During the summer of 1832 he had several acres of cleared land and a commodious frame house built. He fled to this house to escape the epidemic of Cholera which was then raging in Little York.

In 1833, he bought 200 acres adjoining his grant on the Don for which he paid 500 pounds. He built a saw mill, the excavations of which are still in evidence by the old course of the Don within a stone's throw of de Grassi Hill on Don Mills Road.

On April 4, 1833, while he was in Toronto, his house was burnt to the ground in ten minutes, leaving him with the clothes on his back and his family almost nude. Captain de Grassi describes this incident which bespeaks of iron hardship: *'While the house was burning some of my neighbours offered their services to save the furniture, etc., but they kindly saved only the wine of which they freely partook and soon became so drunk as to unable to be of any service.'*
73

East Don Valley up from forks looking west. Note wooden bridge on Don Mills Road over C.N.R.

'In this fire I lost my furniture, clothing, complete silver dinner service, complete service of costly china and a supply of provisions for six months with money and jewelry.'

'In 1834, finding expenses heavy and being unable to carry on the saw mill, I rented it for twenty-five pounds a year. Then another stroke of my old misfortune befell me and as misfortune seldom comes alone, to crown all, the man to whom I had rented the mill ran away, leaving his rent unpaid...I had a short time before erected a stable for my horses and having no other shelter in the wilderness I was glad to live in the stable and one of my children was literally born in a stable and laid in a manger.'

'After the fire I managed amidst great trials and difficulties to struggle on until that unfortunate rebellion broke out in 1837 when Mr. W.L.Mackenzie thought to take upon himself more than regal functions and declared that my property with that of many other loyal men should be parcelled out among his followers.'

Today thousands of motor cars speed daily along the road where de Grassi once trudged with a heart filled with ruin. His mill is gone, although one of his dwellings and the cottage of a son still bear witness to the seasons' changes amid scenery which is loath to part with the past.

The story of the paper mill by the forks of the Don has already been related in 'The Cardinal'. A few foundations tell at least where it once stood by the west Don near the forks.

And what of the forks of today? The clapboard house built by the Taylor's, occupied by Robert Davies from 1890 to the turn of the century, is still standing. It is all that remains to mark the site of the once prosperous Thorncliffe farm. All other buildings and stables have disappeared, only a dwelling or two remain of the village of a century ago. On the grassy slopes to the north of the clapboard house still struggle the remnants of the Davies and Taylor apple orchards.

Near Don Mills Road c.n.r. highway bridge on the west side of de Grassi hill stands a small frame cottage. The house was moved there when the railway went through. In the dreamy days of horse and buggy travel this frame dwelling was known as the de Grassi house. Alexander William James de Grassi, m.d., lived there.

At the foot of de Grassi hill on the east side of Don Mills Road stands another frame building; undoubtedly the de Grassi house which followed the fire of 1834. Mrs.William T. Taylor, who was 90 years of age in 1947, recalled that the house was standing when she was a little girl. On Don Mills Road near this dwelling is to be seen the Club house of the Don Valley School of Art.

Twenty-five years ago, a well-kept rustic bridge spanned Silver Creek, then truly Silver; a road crossed the creek from the cement arch 'White' bridge and continued up a long slope in the valley wall to the Taylor farm, better known as Sam Mayne's farm; today Parkview Hills. The road used by Taylor's wagons and Mayne's trucks has been sealed off. It is gradually returning to the woods. The bridge over the creek has fallen apart. The adjoining meadows are thick with weeds and increasing underbrush. Silver Creek reeks with the odor of sewage.

In all the forks of the Don, one dwelling only has marched benevolently with time and has prolonged its youth. It is the little cream, red-peaked roof cottage which stands on a plateau overlooking the East branch of the Don near the forks. It was built in 1899 by John H.Taylor for farm hands who worked his farm adjoining the pine clad slopes of the valley. A large wooden Cardinal in its peak proclaims that it has survived to see better times. Near the cottage, swathed in encompassing foliage, stands a rustic log cabin. Over the door appears this inscription 'Don Haven, the Home of 'The Cardinal'.'

Fall

THE WEED SEEDS are the hiker's Fall companion. They adhere to his clothing. One travels far before shaking them off. The pods of the Milkweed have burst open, thousands of little parachutes ready to take wing to 'distant lands'. It is the plant's form of migration, as steady and purposeful as the journey of a bird. Bulrushes are spun to a mass of brown cotton on every rush. There are no pickers, save the hands of the wind, which will spin the substance in their own fashion after a while. The haws, the first of the wild apples, are searched out by small birds roaming in bands. The brook, framed in fallen leaves, journeys over variegated formations, some symbolizing quietude through quiet waters, some turbulence through tiny rapids. The stream is an hour glass which never runs out.

No avenue offers more entertainment than a woodland bordering on a meadow. Each flower stalk, tree, shrub, has its own wares, offering them to the eye which travels slowly past. It is the merchandise of the season, leafage in colour, or green. Nature can decorate her windows to the envy of man. Nearby, a small field of hundreds of ripe pumpkins. Pots of pulpy gold.

Old Friends of the Don Valley

JOHN MCARTHUR SR. moved to the Don Valley in 1880 and became one of its first conservationists. He was a beeman. A friend gave him a pound of Bokara Clover seed gathered in the Holy Land. McArthur planted the seed. After several years he considerably multiplied the quantity and began to sow it throughout the valley, particularly along railway embankments, to hold the soil from erosion. The tall tasselled growth sprang up everywhere. Soon McArthur was able to gather thirty bushel bags of clover seed which he sold to the United States Government for ranching crop purposes in the Dakotas.

John McArthur Sr. is survived by John Jr. also a beeman and living in the Don Valley near his apiary at the entrance to Rosedale ravine. John Jr. has the soul of a poet. His familiarity with the Don Valley produced many verses. The clear brook misnamed 'Mud Creek' inspired these lines

My little stream so tightly bound
In ice so cold and crystal clear
Along your banks I've often found
That music floated to my ear.

When a Buttonwood tree was cut down McArthur commemorated the event with these words:

'By the bend of the river Don
Where Mud Creek meanders on,
To join the waters from the north,
There grew a Buttonwood tree.
That as always dear to me
Though I did not know its worth.
But one day men on a survey,
Running a line for a railway,
Into its centre drove a stake.
Then men with axe and saw, ·
When the river was in thaw,
Cut down and floated to the lake.
When it was sawed and planed,
Found so smooth and even grained,
For interior decorating it was sold,   And built into a hall of fame
That will always bear its name,
Written in letters of gold.'

Event after event: Spring, morning, mists, arrival of birds, the visit of a friend, the encroachment of the city; all helped to fill McArthur's book of poems; recording the march of the seasons, the events of his life in the valley which he loved from childhood.

Pottery Road got its name from Burns Pottery. It was in operation at the turn of the century in the valley near the bridge where Pottery Road crosses the Don. Today only a few remnants of pottery remain to mark the site. Across the road 'up valley' from the ruins of Burns Pottery, stood the apiary of J.Rice Murphy, who died in 1952. 'Murph' as he was generally known, lived in a trailer close to his beehives. His disregard for the show of this world's goods was merely a mask for an intelligent perception of basic values. He has been described as the 'Bard of Avon'. I knew him as a philosopher, a man of scrupulous honesty; an idealist. His cabin was littered with the literature of the masters. Despite his seeming aloofness from the world 'Murph' kept a keen interest in current events. For many years

Murphy's tall lithe figure was a familiar one to hikers in the Valley.

Although Fred W.Browne, presently of Leaside, never lived in the Don Valley, he spent much time there, conscious of its recreational value to a growing city. During the depression, unemployed men from all parts of Canada, as it is well known, were so reduced in circumstances as to find it necessary to sek shelter in the brick kilns of the Don Valley Brick Works. Before the end of the depression the flats to the south of the brick works were congested with a mushroom colony of the most makeshift of shelters. The place became known as 'The Jungle'. Every freight train coming down the Don valley in those days had its quota of 'displaced' men riding the box cars to the common place of meeting near Pottery Road.

Unqualified for relief, these unfortunates had to live as best they could. Foremost among their benefactors was Fred W.Browne, often quoted in the newspapers of those days in terms which bespoke of free gifts of blankets, of clothing, of food hampers, of the left overs, brought by Browne to the indigents of the 'Jungle'. One of Browne's prized possessions (a travesty of poverty in the midst of wealth) is a *card of thanks* produced on old cardboard, containing several sheets of writing paper, bound in the form of a brochure. Dated August 4, 1931, it reads:

'To whom it may concern, this is to say that we dwellers of the Don flats, otherwise known as the cave and shack dwellers, do hereby wish to thank all those who have tried to help us out in any way and particularly those kind enough to send any supplies in way of food left over from picnics, etc., which might otherwise have gone to waste and will be glad to accept in future any kindness that this notice might happen to bring us. Hoping things will soon be better we remain thankfully yours.'
Signed below, representing approximately three hundred men: John O'Brien, J.J.Nelson, Harry Morris, Andrew Graham, James Murray, Peter Smith, George Davis, John McDonald, L.Collins, A.Stewart, J.Lafferty, P.Murphy, Peter MacDonald, F.Chambers, J.McConville, Bert Wooten, L.P.Flack.'

Eventually a major exodus was arranged to conduct the men to work camps in the North. The 'Jungle' soon became a jungle of weeds, but to many men, the memory of Fred W.Browne's kind actions lingered on.

Note: Fred W.Browne has already contributed over one hundred dollars to the D.V.C.A.

The Helliwell's

AS ONE WALKS DOWN POTTERY ROAD from Broadview Avenue, there appears in the valley to the left of the road, but several hundred feet to the south of it, a square plan house, with high-peaked roof and overhanging eaves. This familiar landmark has been standing in the Don Valley for one hundred and eighteen years. It is known as *the Helliwell* or *'Mud' House*.

About one hundred feet east of the house stands a ramshackle building with dilapidated brick walls surmounted with a makeshift roof. Its foundations are of river stones. These walls are all that remain of Helliwell's one-time prosperous brewery. Near Pottery Road stands a clapboard cottage, in full view of both the 'Mud' House and the brewery. This frame dwelling was built probably in 1796, by Parshall Terry. William Lea, an early settler on the Don, relates that Parshall Terry lived on a high part of the flats, in a large bend of a hill called 'Terry's Field'. The original 'Terry's Field' was on the site of the Sun Brick Co. quarry, later used as a municipal dump, situated across the Don from the present Beechwood Drive. 'His frame house', related Mr. Lea, 'was moved by Eastwood and Skinner and rebuilt at the Don Mills, remaining there on the estate of the late Thomas Taylor.'

Parshall Terry, a sergeant in Butler's Rangers, had secured large grants of land on the Don. He married into the Skinner family and operated with them a saw and grist mill which stood in 1796 near Pottery Road, opposite Fantasy Farm. (See The Cardinal, December 15th, 1952 issue.)

In time, the saw and grist mill passed from the ownership of the Skinners. Their successor, George Casner, a miller, operated te mills from 1814 to 1820, when Helliwell and Eastwood came on the Don. Thos. Helliwell immediately commenced making brick and preparing for the building of a brewery and distillery. He started brewing and distilling in 1821.

The brewery, the first on the Don, had a capacity for making one hundred and twenty bushels of mash from three to five times a week. It also included a malt house. Rye whiskey was the leading product of the distillery. Helliwell's hop gardens were maintained by settlers from Kent, England. The Helliwell holdings included a cooper's shop, cattle sheds, stables and piggeries.

The story of Tyler and his famous canoe is a colourful remnant of Helliwell history. This Joseph Tyler, 'an old New Jersey man of picturesque aspect' is supposed to have served in the American army during the war of

Section of the Lower Don Valley adjoining Pottery Road. Photo secured in 1938 looks south towards Chesterville Road. Foreground shows an old Don Valley residence in first stages of changeover to 'Fantasy Farm'. Extreme right centre, part of Taylor Brothers 'lower' paper mill. Note bridge spanning Don between Willow trees. Parshall Terry's cabin (not shown in picture) stands near automobile, extreme left side of photo. Remnants of Helliwell's bush are shown below Chesterville Road in background.

Independence. His name is recorded at Newark (Niagara, June 18th 1795). He lived near the Don in a cave on a steep hill, where the General Steelware plant now stands. He is reputed to have introduced the 'sweet edible' Indian corn to Toronto, and probably tobacco as well.

His great canoe made him locally famous. In Tyler's time, Broadview Avenue (The Mill Road), was a tract of White Pine. In these woods Tyler felled, shaped and hollowed out two pine logs, forty feet long, 'fastened together by cross dovetail pieces.'

In the finished craft Tyler poled himself 'down the windings of the Don' to the bay, then to Caroline Street (Sherbourne) where he sold the produce of his garden; also stacks of pine knots, ready split and used as light-jacks for fishermen. On occasion, he ferried people across the Don.

In the Spring of the year when the mill road was a quagmire, the Helliwells engaged Tyler and his canoe to transport their beer to the bay.

'The Lady of the Don', for such the craft was called, took on a cargo of 'twenty-two barrels of beer,' two rows of eleven barrels each, laid lengthwise, side by side, with room to spare for Tyler and a helper to navigate the dugout in the heavy flow of a Spring freshet. The journey down the Don and into the bay, ended at Helliwell's wharf located on the waterfront between Market and Church Streets.

The Helliwell 'Mud' House is the third and last of Helliwell Don Valley residences. The first was a frame dwelling built by the original Thomas Helliwell, Sr. It stood near the brewery and was later torn down. A house built of stone took its place. It was destroyed by fire. The 'Mud ' House was built by William Helliwell in 1837 and was occupied by him until 1847 when he moved to Highland Creek. The 'Mud' House was given that name because it was made of mud bricks of unfired clay, bonded with straw and twigs. It is presently occupied by Mrs. Marjorie Elliott, who operates a pottery studio in the old dwelling.

William Helliwell, son of the pioneer Thomas Helliwell, recorded many of the scenes of his day. From the door of his brewery he saw at various times bears, wolves and deer, moving about in the adjacent forest. One night, wolves killed a dozen of his sheep. His location in the valley presented difficulties, he relates, 'peculiarly formidable for the new settlers to grapple with from the loftiness and steepness of the hills and the kind of timber growing thereabouts; massive pines for the most part.' He was referring to Pottery Road in its original state.

'In 1831', he also relates, 'Misissauga Indians encamped on the banks of the Don in the immediate vicinity of the Helliwell property. The hills and valleys clothed in luxurious foliage were to be seen from the brewery.' Mr. Leland Taylor, of East York, has in his possession a collection of Indian relics picked up by his father and other persons in the Don Valley. This collection of souvenirs of Indian life includes a stone plow, a tomahawk blade, a flint skinning knife and a large egg-shaped stone which was obviously used to pound corn in the wooden vessel hollowed out for the purpose. Dozens of arrowheads were added to the collection. The plow was found in 1913. Weighing about six pounds, it was fashioned to be dragged towards the user in a scraping manner when in operation.

On occasion, Sir Peregrine and Lady Sarah Maitland, the then Lieutenant-Governor of the Province and his wife, visited Helliwell's. The valley of the Don reminded Lady Sarah of her English home 'Goodwood'.

John Eastwood (pioneer paper maker on the Don) wa struck with the resemblance of the Pottery Road section of the Don Valley to Todmorden, England, and thereupon bestowed that name upon it. Mrs. Simcoe refers to the area in these lines: *'I descended the hill and walked to Skinner's Mill through meadows which looked like the meadows of England.'* Dr. Henry Scadding in his writings, describes this part of the valley as *a bower of unspoiled loveliness.*

Thomas Helliwell, Sr., the pioneer Helliwell on the Don, was born in Todmorden, Yorkshire, and as related, came to the Don Valley in 1820. He had previously resided at Lundy's Lane, Ontario, then later at Drummond-

Two photos, courtesy of Jim Salmon, show Helliwell house at turn of the century. The house derived its name from the mud bricks of unfired clay with which it was made.

ville, Quebec. He came to the Don Valley with a family of five sons: Thomas, John, Joseph, William and Charles, also two daughters; Betty who married John Eastwood, and Mary who became the wife of Colin Skinner. The original settlement in the Don Valley adjoining Pottery Road, was one of inter-married families, who were also associated in the same pioneer industries.

The move from Niagara to the Don was made in winter. 'Mrs. Helliwell travelled in a great copper cauldron used for brewing beer, with her youngest son Charlie on her knees. The cauldron was placed on a flat sleigh and drawn by four oxen all the way round from the head of Lake Ontario.'

After the death of Thomas Helliwell, Sr., in 1825, his sons Thomas and William managed the brewery. This arrangement continued until 1840 when Mrs. Helliwell retired from the business. In 1843, the firm became known as Thomas Helliwell and Brothers, directed by Thomas, Jospeh and William. The Toronto office of the firm stood on the south-west corner of King and West Market Streets.

William Lea who lived in the valley at the time of the Helliwell's, affirms that *'in 1838, a flour mill was erected by the firm of Thomas Helliwell and Brothers, who were then employing twenty men, and using 35,000 bushels*

Taylor's Mill Race on Pottery Road. Extreme left centre of photo shows a wooden bridge over the Don, which is today spanned with a concrete structure. This photo secured probably in the 1890's reveals the sylvan character of the lower Don Valley at the turn of the century. Lad is seen fishing in Mill Race. This mill race was probably in use as early as 1783, having been made originally by the Skinners to supply water power for the first saw and grist mill in Lower Don Valley. First tree in left background is a Sycamore, a species once plentiful in the Valley, now, rarely seen.

of barley and rye and grinding 40,000 bushels of wheat a year. Their first mill was built on the Don, below the brewery.'

In 1847 a fire completely destroyed the premises. 'The buildings were erected again and the business went on as usual. The business of manufacturing starch was also carried on, for a sample of which a diploma was given at one of the fairs. Finally, the business fell into the hands of Joseph Helliwell's sons, and in a few years ceased altogether.'

Up until 1880, 'Helliwell's bush' was a well-known name and place. It covered the flats east of the Don lying between the present Prince Edward Viaduct and Pottery Road. Fragments of the bush still cling to the heavily-wooded slopes dominated by Chesterhill Road; the only remaining place where 'Skunk Cabbage' plants are to be found in quantity in the lower Don Valley.

'Helliwell's Bush,' an old-timer related at the turn of the century, *'has nearly all been cut down and the old boys would not recognize the place.*

Shinneys (rough hockey sticks) were cut in Helliwell's Bush by the hundreds and so were clothes props.'

For many years, picnic parties from the city travelled up the Don by row boat to Helliwell's. Here, a spring which still flows from an iron pipe, was considered a major attraction.

Miles and Company, Atlas of 1878, contains this reference to the natural beauty of Pottery Road in its heyday: 'A road leading from Todmorden across the River Don and over the valley to the 2nd concession road east of Yonge Street is particularly beautiful. The devious and narrow way up and down hills is highly interesting and enables the traveller to see the choicest bit of scenery to be found in the neighbourhood of Toronto.'

And today? The valley as seen from Broadview Avenue near Pottery Road is a foliage-encased panorama in which still appear the Helliwell House, the brewery, Taylor Brothers 'lower' paper mill, Whitewood's Riding School and Fantasy Farm. In the background, the 'half-mile' bridge of the C.P.R. spans the valley. Beyond it are to be seen the buildings, chimneys and pit of the Toronto Brick Co.

The artist, T.V.Martin, produced an oil painting of Pottery Road before the turn of the century. Pine trees grace the slopes bordering Hillside Drive. In the painting, haystacks dot meadows where meadows have long since given way to patches of weeds and willows.

Spring 1954

Milne's Hollow

IN THE LATE WINTER OF 1816-17, a strange cortege could be seen travelling from Niagara Falls to York (Toronto). Alexander (Daddy) Milne guided his sleigh and team of horses over the snow-covered backwoods roads. His wife, bundled up against the weather, was seated in a large dyeing kettle. There was other evidence on the sleigh of "Daddy" Milne's dual intention to settle near York and to erect a woollen mill of which the community was in real need.

Alexander Milne was born in Forfarshire, Scotland, in 1777. He immigrated to the United States in 1801. On the recommendation of the British Consul he came to Canada in 1817, to settle on the east half of lot 5, Concession 2, in what was then known as East York.

Before the close of the year 1817, Alexander Milne started to erect a mill on a tributary of the west branch of the Don (Milne's Creek). This creek flows through "Springbrook," the property of Mr. R.E.Edwards, on Lawrence Avenue East, immediately west of Leslie Street extension. The Milne mill stood on the east side of the stream at the foot of a low bluff in the ravine wall at "Springbrook." The site is in full view of Lawrence Avenue. A few years ago, Mr. Edwards removed some of the timbers of the mill dam which were still embedded in the river bank.

An acre of land at the top of the bluff contains the private burying plot of the Milne family. In the shadow of an immense Oak tree, overlooking the site of the mill, lie the remains of the Milne pioneers. Their colourful history is recalled in the fragments of pioneer occupancy: the old well is still on the property in view of Mr. Edward's residence; also Bellflower apple trees of tremendous girth.

The first Milne mill was a three-storey structure. The two lower floors were used for carding and pulling wool. The upper storey was used as a saw mill. The mechanism of the mill was driven by an overshot paddle wheel, 18 feet in diameter). (The name overshot refers to the manner in which the water entered the buckets of the paddle wheel.) Eventually, the small tributary of the Don became insufficient to supply a flow of water large enough to turn the mill wheel. Mr. Milne thereupon moved to a new location on the east Don River, where Lawrence Avenue East now crosses the east valley of the Don.

His second woollen mill was a long rambling single storey building with an overshot paddle wheel fifteen feet in diameter at one end of it. On the opposite side of the Don, a saw mill was built. A single dam supplied water for the two separate mill races required for the two mills. During the great flood of 1878, the saw mills, the logs in the mill pond and the woollen mill were swept away.

A third mill was erected by the Milne's. This mill stood in Milne's Hollow in the east Don Valley until 1946, when it was demolished for the materials which it contained. It was a massively built structure, 80 feet long, 50 feet wide and 40 feet high. It contained three full storeys and a basement with casements well above the ground. A belfry had been built in the centre of the peaked roof. The walls were made of red and yellow brick supported by stone facings. The entire structure rested on stone blocks, three feet thick. A ground-level opening in the form of an arch, was built on the west side of the basement. There were similar openings on each of the three main floors, left there presumably for the purpose of hoisting materials up the mill walls to the interior.

Shafts and pulleys were suspended from the ceilings; all three floors of the building were braced with massive beams of oak. The walls were of plaster and contained numerous windows. At the end of the mill, nearest the mill race, stood an outside area-wall of masonry. It held the turbine in place. This turbine set in motion by the waters of the Don, turned the main shaft, pulleys and belts, which gave the mechanism of the mill its power.

Page 26 of "Illustrated Historical Atlas of Canada and York", published in 1878, carried a sketch of this mill, describing it as Milne-Ford Woollen Mill. The present extension of Lawrence Avenue East, which still winds through the Don Valley, is shown in its original state. Directly on the corner of one of the turns of the road, stood a house with "rough cast" walls: a row of Spruce trees spread their shade in front of the house. This was "Daddy" Milne's residence. To the rear of it could be seen his barns and beyond them, an orchard of Apple and Plum trees of which a few decrepit survivors remain to this day.

Along the road, a short distance from the house, could be observed many years ago, a store operated by "Daddy" Milne and his wife. Near this store the Milne dam spanned the Don. The road pursued its way, over the top of the dam, to the east side of the valley.

The dam commanded a full view of the mill; also of the frame houses scattered about the hollow. In a shed on the east side of the hollow were manufactured buggies, carriages, sleighs, hay-racks, wagons and wooden cisterns.

The scene, in the neighbourhood of the woollen mill, in its hey-day was a lively one; old timers affirm that droves of sheep were washed in the Don before shearing. Wool was to be seen drying on the tenter boards, near the drying shed across the road from the mill. Inside the mill could be heard the movement of the spindles and of the loom. A machine called the Picker, tore the wool to shreds. The Carding machine combed out the fluff. A Fulling machine, used to shrink the wool, contained two alternating beams which pushed the wool to and fro in the water. A descendant of the Milne family relates that the urchins of his time amused themselves by riding back and forth in these "walking" beams.

The third Milne mill closed down in the early 1900's. during the proprietorship of Charles Milne, son of William Milne, and grandson of Alexander Milne.

From within the building, where once was heard the hum of machinery and the softer hum of voices conducting the business of the mill, there came with abandonment, the solace of only one tiny note; that of a tinkling spring, carried by a pipe through the basement wall.

Milne's Hollow, as I first knew it, was sleepy hollow; a place of rank undergrowth, weeds, decrepit barns, sagging dwellings, of fruit trees overgrown with sucker shoots, of tall Elms. Until a few years ago, the disused mill was still standing. The millpond had disappeared long before. The shallow trench of the mill race filled with dormant water covered with algae is still to be seen. "Daddy" Milne's house was destroyed by fire during the Spring of 1921. The tapering Spruce trees which once kept it company have been cut down. The denuded hillsides of old photos, are in the scene of today, covered with tall forest growth. Where once "Daddy" Milne sold oats by the barrel, wild oats now grow in profusion and the Teasel which once served to raise a nap on Milne's woollen cloth now raises itself in successive generations, wuite undisturbed. Today, a stronger traffic bridge replaces the bridge and the road over the dam, washed away by floods so many years ago. The wooden dwellings of the mill workers, in use by other tenants over the years, were demolished early in 1953.

Milne Mill as it was in 1940. It was demolished shortly afterwards for its timber and metal content. A spring flowed from a pipe in the basement.

Time and time again, I wandered through the fine old structure, drinking the spring water which issued from the basement wall; admiring the strength of the wooden gears; examining the oak beams; curiously amused at the handwritten notes, scribbled on the walls by employees long ago: pine beams measuring 60 feet long, cut in the valley were the admiration of all who saw them.

Often, I gazed from a top storey window, over the tops of surrounding trees, to the more distant valley woods: here was a setting of romantic quiet; of hushed abandon; an antithesis of once bustling activity. During the late Winter of 1945, the woollen mill became my setting for the adventures of two boys in the Don Valley; adventures which culminated in the discovery of a "secret" dyeing formula: fiction with some basis of fact, if one could believe old men's tales; but fiction which provided me with the immeasurable pleasure of dramatizing the grand old ruin of Milne's Mill: a story for future issues of "The Cardinal".

Frank Bater, who operates a general store on Broadview Avenue, sold blankets from the Milne Mill over the counter of his store. Many of these blankets are still in use in East York today.

David Gibson, a relative of Alexander "Daddy" Milne, wrote a friend in Scotland on April 27, 1827. He refers to Alexander "Millen" as a fuller and dyer:

"Daddy" Milne's house as it stood on a bend in the road leading from Lawrence Avenue East to Milne's Hollow.

"He has", he wrote, "200 acres of land, a flour mill with two run of stones, a saw mill, fulling mill, dyeing and clothing works and occupies a store of dry goods and spirituous liquor. His brother used to carry on his selling, dyeing, grist mill and saw mill with the assistance of his family. Peter got married this Spring and they dissolved partnership."

The three Milne mills were symbolic of the woollen mills of the small creeks of Ontario. Through them, the settlers were assured of clothing in exchange for their wool. "Upper Canada can meet English manufacturers in price, and in quality can beat the best importers", read an item of October 21, 1846.

In those days the hard winters and the lack of transportation built up barriers, to the benefit of the local woollen mills. With the advent of the railway, Montreal, New York and Philadelphia came within easy reach of Toronto.

The bells in the belfries of the little Ontario mills figuratively cast their shadows on a changing future, long before they ceased to toll through the pressure of changing economic events. While these conditions happened long before the closing of the third Milne mill, it would seem to us inevitable that it should eventually shut down. We can only regret that the building itself was not spared, to extend its usefulness into the lives of other generations, as a romantic landmark of the past, as a museum, a a recreation centre; indeed for many practical purposes. Today it is gone as so many other of the one-time landmarks of the Don Valley.

The Don school erected in 1853, on the north-east corner of Don Mills Road, at a cost of 84 pounds, was demolished a few years ago. The old landmarks on Lawrence Avenue East are being swept away in a frenzy of bulldozing and building and soon, no one will recognize the area for what it formerly was. The Milne woods with their several centuries' old Beech trees are still intact; also the Maple woods contiguous to them in the Don Valley.

Milne's Hollow has scarcely raised a drowsy weedy head from the "sleepy hollow" atmosphere of other years and perhaps it never will. It may go on as a green oasis of tranquillity where people can find true relaxation, or it may ring with the sound of human endeavour, but of what kind, we do not know.

Still, in the Spring of the year, in the Milne woods, pink and mauve Spring Beauties carpet many acres of forest floor, surging around the trees, glowing in the sunlight, a personification of Spring; overhead perhaps an azure sky; ardent sunshine: a picture not readily forgotten. Across the stream from the woods, under a tangle of weeds and willow lies the debris of the old woollen mill, and below it, still seeping from the ancient pipe in the basement wall, the tiny spring which even "the march of progress" cannot stifle as it pursues its never changing course to the Don by Milne's Hollow.

Winter 1954

The North-West Company
Hogg's Hollow and Chuckle Hollow

A FEW YEARS AGO THE ARTIST, FRED FINLEY, O.S.A., produced an oil painting depicting the manner in which men of the North—West Company pulled their heavy bateaux up the steep cliffs of Hogg's Hollow, after ascending the Don River. The scene is further described in these words:
'Each Spring, in the early nineteenth century, the traders of the great North-West Company of Montreal set out for their posts, scattered far across Canada. When their laden bateaux reached York—now Toronto— the voyageurs turned up the Don River, ascending it until they reached the juncture of the Don and Yonge Street. Here the boats were lashed to wheels and pulled bodily up the old road to the Holland River, where they continued their voyage by water to the West. Thus were trading goods carried far across the continent during Canada's early years.'

These men were en route to the West via the Great Lakes in search of furs. They followed the shoreline of Lake Ontario to a portage point on the 'peninsula' approximately in line with the foot of our present Woodbine Avenue; traversed the bay, entered the Don, rowed up the stream to the 'forks', proceeded up the west branch to Hogg's Hollow. This particular use of the Don as a waterway occurred about the turn of the century. Thus Hogg's Hollow became part of Toronto's history long before the Hollow was known by that name.

The North—West Company was formed in the winter of 1783-4. With the opening of Yonge Street, the voyageurs of this Company began to journey along the north shore of Lake Ontario to York, in preference to the former trade route to Lake Huron via the Ottawa River, or the circuitous route of Lake Erie.

A map included in the D.W.Smith papers shows two portages over the peninsula at York; one was in line with Woodbine Avenue and the other directly south of the Don. Mrs. Simcoe relates having received a birch bark canoe, *'such as used by the North-West Company to transport their goods to the Grand Portage beyond Lake Superior. It requires twelve men to paddle.'*

In a document dated December 2nd, 1793, Governor Simcoe expressed the opinion that the road of communication between York and Lake Simcoe would probably be thickly settled by the end of the summer of 1794: *'There is little doubt but that by this communication the North-West Company will supply themselves with many of their heavy articles instead of the circuitous route of Lake Erie.'*

In Simcoe's opinion, the United States would not enter into competition with Canada for any of the fur trade via Lake Huron because of the Yonge Street route which would be open all year round: *'Goods could be received at York until the end of November, passed over to Matchedash Bay and moved out in the spring.'*

In observations by Isaac Todd and Simon McTavish, it is noted that *'goods for this trade which leave London in the Spring of 1794 are sent to the Indian country in 1795 and their produce in furs does not come back to the above posts until 1796, so that it requires at least two years to obtain those returns and get them down to Montreal.'*

The Gazette of March 9th, 1799, informed its readers that *'the North-West Company had given twelve thousand pounds towards the making of a good road and that the North-West Commerce will be communicated through this place' (York).*

Little has been written of Hogg's Hollow in the very early days of its settlement. It must have presented a formidable obstacle to the men of Berczy's German party and the soldiers of the Queen's Rangers who cut the original trail later known as Yonge Street.

Dr. Henry Scadding (*Toronto of Old*, page 441) describes 'The Hollow' as a difficult descent into the valley of the great west branch of the Don. 'Yonge Street', he writes, 'made a grand detour to the east and failed to regain the direct northerly course for some time. The long inclined 'plains' which were cut into the steep sides of the lofty clay banks, produced a roadway which became indescribably bad after a rainstorm. The stream was crossed on a rough timber bridge, known sometimes as Big Creek Bridge and sometimes as Heron's Bridge.'

Carson Park, named after William Carson, is a picturesque woodland recently acquired by the city. The park is part of Hogg's Hollow and adjoined—when these lines were written-the smooth rolling lawns of York Downs Golf Course. Here the wooded hillsides in a natural state were in sharp contrast to the carpet-like Golf Course. The long forest aisle seen from the bridge spanning Hogg's Hollow appears in folds of inter-lapping hillsides draped with evergreens, simulating the receding scenery of a huge stage of the outdoors. Here is probably the Queen of Vistas of the entire Don Valley ravine system.

Another locally famous 'Hollow' adjoins Don River Drive. It is called Chuckle Hollow and is on the property presently owned by Mr. Paul Hinder, Lot 17, Concession I, York. Its fame dates back to the Rebellion of 1837.

After the debacle at Montgomery's Tavern, Wm.Lyon Mackenzie made his way to Shepard's Mill in Chuckle Hollow. He was closely pursued by the 'King's Men'. The soldiers were persuaded that Mackenzie could not make his escape during the night, as they had the hollow surrounded at all points with the exception of a steep almost sheer cliff, rising from the shores of the Don opposite the mill. No one would climb the cliff, so they thought.

During the darkness, one of Mackenzie's followers led a horse to the edge of the cliff, tied a rope to the animal and lowered the rope down the cliff. Mackenzie dressed as a woman, so the tale goes, was pulled to safety and to freedom. I have been unable to verify this rebellion of 1837 tale. The late Wm.Lyon Mackenzie King with whom I had correspondence on the subject could not confirm it. The story persists. In his book 'All the King's Men', Stephen Neil relates: 'The rumour was never refuted that Mackenzie escaped and disguised in the garments of a servant girl.' 'Humours of 37' by Lizard also mentions Mackenzie's escape in the disguise of a woman. Some persons are of the opinion that the soldiers were just as well pleased to see Mackenzie on his way.

Mackenzie left us his own story about his visit to Chuckle Hollow. 'Finding myself closely pursued and repeatedly fired at, I left the high road with one friend, Mr. J.R., and made for Shepard's Mills. The fleetest horsemen of the official party were as close to upon us that I had only time to jump off my horse and ask the miller himself (a Tory) whether a large body of men, then on the heights, were friends or foes, before our pursuers were climbing the steep ascent almost beside me.'

This account tells us positively that Mackenzie was at Chuckle Hollow, where Shepard's Mills were located. Records show that Jos.Shepard operated a saw mill on Lot 16 and Michael Shepard a grist mill on Lot 17, Concession I, West of Yonge Street. The name is spelled differently on several maps. Mackenzie spelt it in the same manner as shown on old maps locating the position of the mills.

Whether Mackenzie's escape was precipitated by the sensational pursuit which he describes or undertaken in the less dramatic disguise of a woman has not been determined. Nevertheless, his presence in Chuckle Hollow has left us with a fragment of history which we would not otherwise have had.

Winter 1954

Salmon in the Don

MR.C.R.NASH, PROVINCIAL BIOLOGIST at Toronto, told the Toronto Field Naturalists Club in 1924 that the last salmon to be found in the Don had been speared with a pitch fork under the Dam at Taylor's Mill (Pottery Road) '40 or 50 years ago.' That is to say in 1874 or perhaps a few years earlier.

John Smith who lived near the mouth of the Don River in 1852 saw his last salmon in the Don in that year. When the Simcoe's came on the Don in 1793, many salmon were speared in the river near Castle Frank, or slightly below the present Prince Edward viaduct. Captain John Playter, also a settler of 1793, on one occasion took from the Don ninety salmon near Castle Frank.

Much later, the annual catch of salmon in the Don, according to Dr. Scadding, still amounted to many hundreds of fine fish. He saw twenty heavy salmon speared within an hour. The following picturesque description of salmon fishing on the Don is from his writings: 'At certain seasons the salmon was to be captured in the Don, and a solitary canoe was now and then to be seen, proceeding on its way, bearing a genuine Red man of the forest in quest of this fish; after nightfall a torch of burning pine knots making him all the more noticeable. Good fish besides salmon were numerous. Spring water rivulets entering the main stream at several points were frequented by Speckled trout.'

William Lea describes the Don in the year 1821 as a river 'inhabited by various kinds of fish; large quantities of suckers in the early Spring and in the latter part of the Summer by the finest salmon which were taken in great numbers sometimes weighing 25 pounds each.'

In Mr. Lea's descriptive comments of the salmon run on the Don, we read:

'They were caught by being trapped under the mill dams and water wheels of the mills, but were generally caught with a spear with prongs of steel, barbed near the points (resembling Neptune's trident) with a socket, and for the pole, a piece of white ash ten feet long. A skiff was used with a place in the bows for the light jack, a sort of fork, so as to swing and keep the right side up. This was fixed to the bow of the boat, filled with pitch pine and set on fire, giving a very bright light while his mate or assistant sat at the stern and paddled and steered the boat. The fish could be seen at a very considerable distance distinctly when the water was not too deep. Salmon have disappeared through want of protection.'

The protection of salmon to which Mr. Lea refers (conservation in our day), was a cause of concern to public-spirited citizens as early as 1799. On April 27th of that year, a motion was made in the council office of York to subject the purchase of the grist mill seat on the Humber to the conditions that the full passage of fish up and down the river would not be obstructed in any manner. The motion was this worded:

'The lessee to take all other necessary measure for preventing the fish being destroyed in the mill race by the mill wheel or otherwise, by erecting and maintaining in good repair proper racks for that purpose. That wicker steps shall be placed above the mill race to prevent the salmon being drawn into the stream and either brought within the race of cut to pieces by the wheel. That a free passage shall be left for the salmon and other fish to descend the river.'

The same precautions were meant to apply to the Don and other nearby streams. They were not adhered to, for the destruction of the salmon continued; a tragic disappearance to which we find this reference in 'The Valley of the Humber':

'At the beginning of the last century salmon were numerous in proportion to the size of the rivers as they are now in British Columbia. They were doomed to destruction because every settlement demanded a grist mill and saw mill, the mills required dams and no salmon could pass to the spawning ground except the few that survived the gauntlet of the mill races. They crowded at the foot of the dams and as every settler had a spear they were slaughtered wholesale. Those that escaped the spear were taken by gill net in thousands; the numbers gradually decreased, and in the sixties they were exterminated.' Dr. J.H.Richardson who penned the above lines consideres that the wholesale destruction in the welter at the foot of the dams as part self-inflicted: 'fighting and the madness to reach the spawning ground led to unmeasured damage.'

The first settlers in Ontario believed that the salmon which spawned in the rivers flowing into Lake Ontario came all the way from the Atlantic Ocean. Dr.J.H.Richardson in 'University Monthly' January 1908, tells us 'Don River salmon were 'lake-locked' and never migrated to the sea.' Dr.W.J.K.Harkness, Director of Ontario Department of Fish and Wild Life, whose article on salmon appeared in the 'Toronto Star' of August 6th, 1947, says on the subject: 'Once Lake Ontario was noted for its land-locked salmon. These were exactly the same as those in the ocean, but were trapped or lost in Ontario and lived out their natural lives there. Until about 1880 these salmon were fairly abundant in Lake Ontario and then mysteriously disappeared.' An advertisement in the Gazette of May 16th, 1798, provides an interesting item concerning the presence of salmon on the Don. It reads: 'To be sold by public auction on Monday the 2nd of July next, at John McDougall's hotel, in town of York, a valuable farm, situated on Yonge street, about twelve miles from York, on which are a good loghouse and seven or eight acres improved. The advantages of the above farm, from the richness of its soil and its being well watered, are not equalled by many farms in the province; and above all, it affords an excellent salmon fishery large enough to support a number of families.

Winter 1954

The Passenger Pigeon

NO STORY OF THE DON WOULD BE COMPLETE without some mention of the passenger pigeon. As the salmon disappeared from the Don River, the Passenger pigeon has disappeared from the woods and skies of the Don Valley where it was once seen in astronomical numbers.

On April 10th, 1796, Mrs. Simcoe observed that the air was full of pigeons as she walked to Castle Frank. *'The flights of wild pigeons in the Spring and Autumn is a surprising sight'* she records elsewhere in her diary. *'They fly against the wind and so low that at Niagara the men throw sticks at them from the fort and killed numbers. The air is somewhat darkened by them...they build where there are plenty of acorns but do not feed within twenty miles of the place, reserving that stock of provisions till the young ones can leave their nests, and then scratch the acorns for them.'*

Pioneers frequently commented upon the Passenger pigeons of their day, One man saw a new-sown field blue with them. In other instances the pigeons were observed in mass flights stretching across the horizon as far as the eye could reach. Settlers shook young squabs off the limbs of trees by the dozen. The fmaous naturalist, Ernest Thompson Seton gave an account of the last great flight seen over Toronto and the Don Valley.

'In those days the most conspicuous and abundant of wild life around us was the huge flocks of wild pigeons that came over in the Spring and Fall. All of my school friends reckoned on the pigeon shooting as the most thrilling of the wildwood pastimes. I shall never forget the last great horde that passed over, it was in 1876 about April 20th. An army of pigeons flew overhead due north. The flocks seemed only about twenty deep but extending east and west as far as could be seen fading into a smoky line on each horizon. There must have been hundreds of thousands in that flock and it was succeeded by others of similar extent every half-hour for most of the day. I saw it all from my bedroom window and I must sorowfully add that it

was the last of the great flocks that, according to record, ever came over Toronto.' Seton lived a stone's throw from the Don Valley in 1876.

A flock of pigeons seen in Kentucky in 1808 was estimated at two billion. The naturalist Audubon told of flights so dense that they darkened the sky. The slaughter of these birds presaged their extermination before the turn of the twentieth century. The depletion of the forests and consequential eliminating of natural food helped to further decrease their numbers. Their destruction pursued its course to the elimination of a last single specimen which died in a Cinncinati zoo in 1912. Since then a reward has been offered to anyone who may locate a single survivor of the species.

And so, the salmon and the Passenger pigeon at one time abundant along the Don have gone their way never to return. Man may yet learn the lessons of the past; life is not inexhaustible, once extinguished in one particular species he is powerless to restore it.

<hr>

Summer 1954

<hr>

The Old Belt Railway and Seton's 'Glenyan'

ABOUT THE YEAR 1891, a project several decades ahead of its time was planned for the Don Valley. This project was known as the Belt Line Railway. The idea is attributed to Henry W.Tyler, then president of the Grand Trunk Railway. It was carried out by superintendent James Stephenson. Mr.Tyler believed that the route would be a convenient and practical way to route freight around Toronto instead of taking it down in the 'hollow' of the city. It is said that the Belt Line was also planned to provide transportation in support of a land boom, then affecting the north end of the city of Toronto. The Don Valley and Moore Park ravine, also known locally as 'Cudmore's' and 'Mud Creek' ravine were convenient arteries along which to lay a section of the line.

A letter in my files from Canadian National Railway System gives these facts pertaining to the Belt Line Railway:

'Our first line in the Don Valley was that of the old Toronto Belt Line Railway, which was operated by the Grand Trunk Railway, now part of Canadian National Railways. Our files do not give the exact date of track construction but they indicate that the line was opened for traffic in 1892 and operation discontinued in 1894. A few years later, in 1906, the Canadian Northern Railway, also a part of the present Canadian National System, laid a line in the Don Valley and inaugurated train service from Toronto to Parry Sound.'

A passenger who made the twenty-five mile trip around the Belt Line in

1892 relates that the rails ran along the waterfront from the Don to east of Jane Street and west of the 'factory' at Swansea. Here, they turned north through Home Smith property to Bloor Street. Crossing Bloor, the railway 'cut' Jane Street at this point, continuing north and westerly on the bench of land east of the Humber above the old mill, through the orchard of the Baby family, then past Baby Point, then north-easterly, and east to Yonge Street on the north side of Mount Pleasant cemetery. The Belt Line then followed the Moore Park ravine to the Don Valley. The route continued down the west side of the Don Valley and Don River to the Esplanade and to the Union Station. The fare was twenty-five cents per trip. The trains ran every hour early and late in the day.

Surprisingly little information is available on the subject of the Belt Line Railway. Up until 1914 the rusty rails and decaying sleepers could still be seen in the sylvan ravine of 'Mud Creek'. I have heard it said that the rails were removed during the first World War to be used as scrap metal. Mr. Herb Staples, son of the late Owen Staples, recalls that the rails were in place in 1912. He also remembers seeing some rusty, old-fashioned locomotives on a siding near the present Brick works.

In less than two years from its inception, the Belt Line Railway was a thing of the past. This seems surprising enough considering its advantages: Toronto was then emerging from the era of its horse-drawn street car days. The Belt Line Railway held the promise of a thrilling twenty-five mile ride around the outskirts of the city and through some of the loveliest ravines. It offered an opportunity for entire families to spend a day in the country, and with ease, considering the frequency of the schedule. To some observers of the 1890's, the project was thirty years ahead of its time. People were obviously not ready for it; a condition reflected in the number of passengers it carried.

Today, the one-time 'right-of-way' of the Belt Line Railway in Moore Park ravine shows the preliminary work of 1946—Prelude to a traffic artery: trees have been cut down, embankments have been built up. Eventually this new artery will convey thousands of motor cars along a route which to the planners of the old Belt Line Railway promised to be a 'great public advantage'.

In 1882 'Picturesque Canada' made this interesting observation in relation to that part of the Don Valley adjoining Moore Park Ravine: 'We continued our ramble through the woods in the direction of Yorkville. Here it is designed to utilize the great natural beauties of the place (Don Valley) by laying out a segment or cordon of parks, which it is hoped will one day surround the city.' Prophetic words in the light of today's 'Green Belt' plan.

In the same publication appears elsewhere these lines: 'But we move on around the hill towards the picturesquw environs of Rosedale. Here the twin valleys of the Don (the writer may have meant Castle Frank ravine and Rosedale ravine) have been spanned by graceful bridges, and the finely wooded plateau has been opened up to the suburban settlement.'

Dying days of a project which promised to be a 'great advantage': The rusty rails and decaying sleepers of Moore Park ravine section of the old Belt Line Railway are shown here — also Moore Park Station. The Station remained standing until the early nineteen thirties. Photo taken in 1907 by Stuart L.Thompson.

Today, suburban settlement extends twenty-five miles beyond this point.

'Mud Creek' Ravine through which the old Belt Line passed, was the background for another event which has contributed to the fame of the Don Valley. In 'Mud Creek' ravine was located the 'Glenyan' of Ernest Thompson Seton's book, 'Two Little Savages'. As a small boy, I came under the spell of this book. First my brothers read it to me, then I read and re-read it with great fondness. Many thousands of boys have done likewise.

In later years, it became apparent to me that the opening chapters of 'Two Little Savages' were based on the Don Valley. Accordingly, I commenced a series of explorations to locate 'Glenyan' and finally came upon the place which answered to the description of 'Glenyan' in 'Two Little Savages'.

This place was in the Belt Line ravine, but reached through a small dale which stood directly across to the west from the present clay pit of the Don Valley Brick Works. On March 17, 1933, I received a reply to a letter to Mr. Seton, from which these extracts are quoted: *'You have pretty well got down to the facts of Glenyan. In my early days in Toronto, that is 1870, the city ended at what was then Cruickshank Street (Dundas Street) which crossed Sherbourne Street between Shuter and Gerrard. Nothing but open fields north of this, although there were plenty of houses on each side of Yonge Street up to Yorkville. Mud Creek ravine was the place I called 'Glenyan' and the exact site of my cabin was just underneath the windows of the present Government House.'*

'I have heard this creek called Cudmore's creek and the hill beyond it on the north Cudmore's Hill. But this was long before any railroad ran through. To a small boy as I was then, it was a far cry into a wild and distant country. To me, it was a paradise. The notorious Brooks gang of outlaws used my shanty in the 70's.'

In Mr. Seton's second letter to me, dated March 7th, 1938, there is a further reference to 'Glenyan': *'The incidents given in 'Two Little Savages' relate to the Don Valley. That is, part one, which deals with 'Glenyan'. The exact site of my shanty was just north of the Government House, that is, tucked under the hill on the level of the bottom land.'*

On June 9th, 1945, I received from Mr. Seton this third and last reference to 'Two Little Savages': *'I shall be glad to have you quote from my 'Two Little Savages'—After the war is over, if I am alive, I shall go to the very spot of 'Glenyan' and put up some sort of a monument. This of course was the beginning of the Boy Scouts.'*

Ernest Thompson Seton died on October 23rd, 1946, at the age of 86. He did not return to 'Glenyan' to put up the monument he had in mind, yet this simple desire revealed the spell which the Don Valley cast upon him all through his years. He rose to the greatest heights of his calling. He became one of the world's great naturalists. He wrote forty-two books, including a nature encyclopedia, but to the last he kept a place in his affections for the valley which had meant so much to him as a boy.

In his 'Trail of an Artist-Naturalist' Mr. Seton dwelt extensively on the background of his adventures in 'Glenyan'. He describes his joy comparable to that of Balboa discovering the Pacific, when he traversed Dundas Street the then northern boundary of the city, to the open fields flanking St. James cemetery, to the wilderness of ravines and thick woods opening out on the Don flats: *'The last outpost of civilization was Drumsnab Castle,'* he relates, *'and far far away was Taylor's Mill.'*

Saturday after Saturday he tramped through this area, travelling ever northward to Taylor's Hill, then westerly following its base, up the third ravine 'and discovered a most glorious wooded glen.'

'Hemlock, Birch, Pine and Elm of the largest size abounded and spread over the clear brook a continuous shade. Fox vines trailed in the open spaces, the rarest wild flowers flourished—the Veery, the Hermit Thrush or even a wood Thrush sang his sweetly solemn strain in that golden twilight of the midday forest.' Seton named it after its discoverer, 'Glenyan'.

Seton the boy kept the secret to himself. He built a cabin there, ten feet long, six feet wide, three feet high at the back. A picture of this cabin with Yan in Indian 'get up' in front of it, is to be seen in *'Two Little Savages'*. Seton was fourteen years of age when he began building it. During most of the year 1874 it was in progress. In the Spring of 1875 he found immeasurable happiness in going to the site of the cabin on Saturdays, alone in terms of human companionship, but overwhelmed with the company of the woods and nature. He imagined himself Robinson Crusoe and Swiss Family Robinson rolled into one, he played Indian and frowned on anything un-Indian like. He cultivated an Indian accent: 'White man heap no good' was a favourite phrase, and how bitterly he may have said it in our day, had he seen his beloved ravine and adjoining valley in their present state.

'All the life went out of me,' he relates when on a last visit to the shanty he saw 'three awful-looking tramps in his cabin playing cards and drinking.' These tramps were members of the notorious Brooks Bush gang who for years terrorized people in the east end of Toronto.

A few days after the incident, 'Yan' returned to the cabin to find his little haven quite destroyed. He abandoned the place shortly afterwards but never to forget it. Even in mature years, Mr. Seton kept alive the coals of memory of those early camp fires in the hidden ravine up the Don.

In November of 1938, he visited Toronto for the last time. He and his nephew Stuart L.Thompson of Toronto, walked out to Governor's Bridge in Rosedale and from the bridge looked along the dale of 'Glenyan'. It was a cold, rainy, wind-driven day; a combination of weather such as to make a visit to the actual site of 'Glenyan' impracticable. As an alternative, the two men walked around into the grounds of Chorley Park to the crest of the ravine. From there, Mr. Seton again pointed out the actual site of his dear to memory cabin: 'Almost as I knew it in 1874,' he said and turned sadly away.

And what of 'Glenyan' today and of its surroundings? The face of the ravine below Chorley Park—the Government House—has been marred with 'fill' from the Toronto subway diggings. The 'right-of-way' of the Old Belt Line Railway, built twenty years after Seton first knew the place, has now been converted, one could say indoctrinated with the first formations of a traffic artery. The 'ever narrowing entrance' by which Seton reached the ravine has disappeared. The silver brook, misnamed in his day 'Mud Creek', is still flowing although reduced in volume and with water at times not crystal clear. Beyond the ravine to the east, lies the immensely gaping pit of the Don Valley Brick works, ever enlarged since 1882. The lower Don Valley has taken on a derelict appearance, compared to the unspoiled beauty of the valley as Seton knew it.

The German Mills

THE GERMAN CREEK flows into the east Don river about a mile and a half north of Oriole. The creek is a mere fingerling of its former self, although its waters were abundant enough in 1794 to convey rafts loaded with the belongings of a party of German settlers. These colonists formed a settlement and built the German mills farther along the creek. The location of the German mills was about a quarter of a mile above Steele's avenue, or more precisely on lot 4, concession three, Markham. The ravine through which the creek flows is partly wooded. A gravel pit has obliterated most of the original site of the mills. An earthen moat is all that remains to mark the contours of the former mill pond. A few boards still protrude from the shores of the creek to indicate some previous construction. Nothing more remains but history, to remind us of the events which once took place there.

The German mills were named from the settlement established in Markham township by William Berczy. The facts of Berczy's entry into Canada are contained in his own narrative on pages 128-129 of the Russell papers and recopied below. He was in New York in February 1794 looking for a place to settle 84 'colonists', meaning families constituting a total of 229 persons, most of whom he had brought out with him from Germany. He petitioned Governor Simcoe for one million acres of waste lands. This petition was dated March 20th, 1794. In mid-April of that year he arrived at Navy Hall, near Newark (Niagara).

'The Government and Council not deeming it consistent to grant at once such a large tract of land resolved upon my declaration that I have sixty heads of families ready to bring immediately into the Province ... to grant me sixty four thousand acres of land with the promise of more land when that first tract should be properly settled. In consequence of which I proceeded to the neighbouring State of New York where my people were waiting for my further dispositions and brought in the month of June, 1794, to Niagara more of the promised sixty heads of families.'

Mr. A.D.Bruce of Unionville is of the opinion that Berczy was joined before entering Canada by a party of Pennsylvanian Dutch settlers.

Berczy's narrative is here resumed: *'I submitted myself cheerfully,'* he wrote, *'to maintain about two hundred people in a distant part of the woods, till I could establish them in the month of November, 1794, on the granted lands twenty miles back from the then beginning town of York.'* That the

Berczy settlement was well established by the end of the year 1794 is also indicated in a letter written under date of November 20th, 1794, by a gentleman then making a tour of Upper Canada. The letter reads: 'On the east side and joining the rear of these lots is a settlement of near 100 German families, on an excellent tract of land, much of which is open white oak woods; these Germans came on this summer furnished with everything to make their situation comfortable... they are supported by a company who have liberally supplied them with teams, farming utensils, and provisions, sent them a clergyman of their own country and are about to build them mills, a church and a school house.' (Simcoe papers).

Mrs. J.B.Coates, a direct descendant of one of the original Eckhardt pioneers of the Berczy group, wrote:
'These settlers came across Lake Ontario on their way to Canada, briging in their stock of animals, household goods, machinery etc., all in one load. They landed a little way up the river Don, about where Queen street now crosses it. The river was much fuller and larger in those days. The surrounding country was solid forest. They used flat bottom boats which drew six inches of water, and the women and children and mill machinery and furniture and animals were sent up the North branch of the Don river to the proposed mill site. The horses and cattle went up Yonge street, blazing a service trail as they went. They were notable mill builders and in the valley of a branch of the Don, two or three miles east of Thornhill, may still be found traces of the tannery, distillery, brewery, sawmill, woollen mill and other buildings which they erected.'

Mr. A.D.Bruce (Historical Sketch of Markham Township) records the statement of Frederic Summerfeldt to the effect 'that many of the company has crossed the lake in 'boats', while others, himself included, went by land around the head of the lake taking with them their live stock.'

Honorable David Wm.Smith the surveyor-general of Simcoe's time refers to the German mills in his Topographical Description of Upper Canada, printed in 1799, where he wrote: 'On the east side of Yonge Street in the rear of York and Scarborough is the township of Markham, settled principally by Germans. In this tract are some good mills, built on a branch of the river Nen (The Don).

A reference to the early settlement of Germans near Toronto, which cannot be ignored, was entered in Mrs. Simcoe's diary on Sunday, Jan. 19th, 1794. She wrote: 'The weather was so pleasant that we rode to the bottom of the bay, crossed the Don, which is frozen, and rode to the Peninsula. Returned across the marsh which is covered with ice, and went so far as the settlements which are near seven miles from the camp. There appeared some confortable log houses inhabited by Germans and some Pennsylvanians.' Who precisely these Germans were, we do not know; an advance party perhaps of the main group which accompanied Berczy to York in the same year. Mr. A.D.Bruce relates that Melchior Quantz, a veteran soldier of a Hessian regiment had been in Markham two years before Berczy arrived. And undoubtedly there were others.

The Cummer house (erected probably in 1794) is all that remains of the German Mills settlement. It stands on a slope overlooking the site of the mills, and is presently inhabited by Mr. Gilbert Clarke, who is married to a descendant of the Cummer family.

This house erected in 1794 by Phillip Eckhardt one of the original settlers at the German Mills, stands on cemetery hill lot 17, concession 6, Unionville. The walls of the house are made of squared timbers. See Historical Sketch of Markham Township, for photo of dwelling showing its original appearance.

A.J.H.Eckhardt, a pioneer, said that the settlers arrived in the Spring of 1794. 'The mills were located about three miles east of Thornhill and three miles west of Unionville.'

This Eckhardt cut practically 'all the timber required for Governor Simcoe's buildings and houses which was floated about twelve miles down the Don river to what was called York in 1792-3-4.'

The following extracts from the Simcoe papers of March 16th, 1794, throw further light on the arrival of the Germans:

'The manager under Mr. Williamson and the whole of the Germans have shown an inclination to emigrate into Upper Canada.' And the additional note: 'William Berczy brought over to York County later in the year 1794, sixty-four German families from the Pulteney Settlement.'

From Navy Hall on June 2nd, 1794, Simcoe wrote another letter on the subject:

'Mr. Bertzie, the German agent for Messrs. Pulteneys is here to obtain a settlement for the Germans.'

The coming of these Germans to Canada created some indignation in the United States. 'The Gazette' published in Philadelphia, commented on the Berczy settlers in its issue of July 25th, 1794, in these words: 'The British have decoyed to their settlements a number of families who were under the most strict obligations to Mr. Williamson whi had advanced them an enormous sum.'

Governor Simcoe took a different view. He said these settlers preferred the British form of Government, and he lists as reasons: the oppression of the land jobbers, the uncertainty of titles, the dread of the Indians.

At first things did not go well with the Berczy settlers. On Feb. 23rd, 1796, Berczy addressed a petition to Simcoe in which he said that many of his associates were almost starving. Some had had not flour since the previous September, their principal subsistence being potatoes and turnips. He requested ten barrels of pork, eighty bushels of peas, 1,300 pounds of rice. Already many of the settlers had left their families to find work and provisions in the Niagara district. Berczy assured Simcoe he had done everything possible to avert this calamity.

On July 14th, 1796, he asked for a prolongation of time for replacing the borrowed provisions. He gave as reason for non-fulfilment of his promise the general scarcity of food: *I could scarcely gather so much as was necessary to bring the people through to now.'*

Berczy had plans much more grandiose than the settling of sixty German families on the Don. He was one of the agents behind a petition for one million acres of land addressed to Governor Simcoe under date of March 20th, 1794. In case two million acres of land were obtained, two hundred thousand acres were to be offered for sale by the company's agents in Germany (Simcoe papers, Vol. 2, page 191). His demands were not met and he became dissatisfied with the conditions in which he and his settlers then found themselves. On August 13th, 1797, after Simcoe had returned to England, Berczy summed up his grievances in a letter to Peter Russell, the new Lieutenant-Governor. In this letter he declared that the Governor-in-Council had granted the German settlers sixty four thousand acres with a promise to grant more land when that tract 'be properly settled'.

'The aforesaid Proclamation to the King's Most Excellent Majesty states that six months after effective settling of tracts of lands or townships, patents or deed should be issued for such granted land.' 'After I had in due time severally applied for these deeds of the granted land I saw after two years residence and work on said land that I could have no deed or grant before an uniterrupted residence of seven years in the Province not being a natural born or naturalized subject of Great Britain.' 'I applied for the first time for a patent in the month of May 1795 ... In the month of October 1796, it was for the first time stated that no deed or grant could be issued before several years uninterrupted residence.'

In this correspondence Berczy again insisted that he had supported the settlers with all of the necessities of life for nearly two years. He asked to have his claims confirmed.

Berczy was a man of unusual ability. He was familiar with the canal system of the American colonies. Because of this, he conceived the idea of laying a canal to connect the Rouge with the Holland river. A map published in 1800 by D.W.Smith the Surveyor-general of the time, shows the location of this project; a canal from the headwaters of the Rouge across the township of Markham and part of Whitchurch to connect with a branch of the Holland river, which rises near the town of Aurora. The canal, as shown on the old map, would have formed a waterway through York county linking Lake Ontario with Lake Simcoe.

In 1799, Berczy, who had been living in York, left the settlement on the German creek to the care of others and retired to Montreal. At that time his loss in the venture was estimated at $150,000. In Quebec Province he employed himself as an architect and painted murals in several churches. Some of his work remains to this day. There are several mentions in the Russell papers of his stay in Quebec. He died in 1830 at the age of sixty-eight.

In 1805 the German mills were advertised in the 'Gazette' to be sold for the payment of debts due to Berczy's creditors. The grist mill was advertised as having 'a pair of French burr stones and complete machinery for bolting superfine flour.' The sale included lots 2 and 4 in the 3rd concession and 300 acres, also lots 31 and 32 in the 2nd concession. The mills were purchased and kept in operation by Captain Nolan of the 70th regiment. The speculation was not a success. The 'Gazette' again announced the sale of the German mills 'and a distillery in operation.'

Doctor Scadding refers to the mills in his 'Toronto of Old'. According to his text, the mills were advertised in the U.C. Loyalist of April 15th, 1828. The property then consisted of four hundred acres of land with good dwelling house, barn, stable, saw mill, grist mill, distillery, brew house, malt house, several other buildings, constituting, observed Dr. Scadding 'a rather impressive sight, coming upon them suddenly in the midst of the woods in a deserted condition, with all their windows boarded up.'

The 'good dwelling house' is still standing, situated on a slope by the road overlooking the site of the mills and the gravel pit which has obliterated most of this site. At this writing it is occupied by Mr. Gilbert Clarke, who married into the Cummer family, the original owners of the dwelling.

Mr. Clarke told me that an earthen moat still visible is all that remains of the one-time contours of a large pond. Clustered around the base of the ravine were the huts of the original settlers, then later the dwellings of the mill workers. Cattle were at one time put on rafts and floated down the German Creek to the Don, then to the Bay. It can be said that practically all of the timber required for Governor Simcoe's buildings and houses were also floated down the Don from the German Mills. The German settlers also helped to clear the bush to make a road for the future Yonge Street.

The de Grassi Homestead
A Conservation Centre in the Making

DON MILLS ROAD winds through the east valley of the Don, crosses the arch bridge at the forks of the Don, then along the road again to a steep grade and the wooden trestle bridge spanning the C.N.R. Don Valley line. This grade is known locally as de Grassi hill.

At the foot of de Grassi hill and nestling in a crook in the east side of the road, stands a frame dwelling. The house stands on land acquired in 1832 by Captain Phillipe de Grassi as part of a government grant. John H.Taylor, who died in 1940 at the age of eighty-seven, told me that his father bought de Grassi's land from him. 'John H.' remembered de Grassi as a tall dark man of whom the children of his time were exceedingly respectful. (See December 15th 1955 issue of 'The Cardinal' for the story of Captain de Grassi.

Mrs. Wm.Taylor, who was ninety years of age in 1947, said that she had spent her life near the Don Valley and the frame dwelling was in her earliest recollections. Wm. de Grassi (one of de Grassi's sons) is listed in the Toronto and City Home District Directory of 1846-7 as residing on lot 6, concession three, the lot on which the old dwelling was erected. These facts and other evidence would indicate that the house at the foot of the hill replaced Phillipe de Grassi's pioneer home, destroyed by fire in 1833. The hand-made laths, the square nails, the one-inch-thick pine planks, measuring sixteen inches wide; the quaint carpentry of the corner joints all point to a type of construction which by our standards would be considered old. I estimate that the dwelling has been standing for 120 years. Another cottage once occupied by the members of the de Grassi family is to be seen on the north side of the railway, directly west of Don Mills road.

I first saw the de Grassi homestead in June of 1921. The lot at that time still had the drowsy air of a pioneer settlement. A shed full of old rusty tools and the accoutrement of by-gone days stood near the house. Another shed was to be seen to the rear of the lot. Across the yard from it on the banks of the Don, Skelhorne's piggery added an unpicturesque note to the decor. Occasionally a motor car of the vintage of the twenties would roll past the house, to slow down into low gear at the first grips with de Grassi hill. Otherwise the tranquillity of the valley was quite undisturbed.

Skelhorne's was a stepping-off for the boys of several scout troops, who left their bicycles in the shed before the trek up the tracks for week-end summer camps. In those days the valley above de Grassi's was truly an unspoiled wilderness.

By 1927, I was established as part-time tenant on the holdings across the stream from Skelhorne's. It did not occur to me then that I would one day own all of the land in the area, including Skelhorne's. As events transpired, Bill Skelhorne moved out of the valley to larger quarters at Wexford. His brother-in-law, Charlie Bell, took over the de Grassi place and the business of raising hogs continued as before. Eventually Bell left the premises. The sound of squealing swine was heard no more: with the porkers went the unpleasant odor of boiling swill and smell of hogs which had so often tainted the valley air, particularly during the dog-days of Summer.

I purchased the property from Canadian National Railways in 1947. The premises were occupied for several years by tenants who treated the beauty of the place with scant consideration.

In September of 1951, a fire broke out in the kitchen and almost sealed then and there the fate of the de Grassi house. I had the place restored, and tenancy resumed its normal course. On the night of October 16th, 1954, the Don rose eighteen feet, swept over the Skelhorne yard to a depth of five feet, leaving in its wake a foot of mud on the floors of the old homestead. The next morning I resolved to turn the place into a Conservation Centre.

In the old days the de Grassi house was several times invaded by flood waters, particularly so during the two great floods of April 1850 and September 1878. In my time the Spring flood of 1929 brought the waters of the Don to the walls of Skelhorne's piggery. The pigs were evacuated in a hurry. The waters receded before reaching the house, although there was some damage to the river bank. Skelhorne filled in the eroded places with several truckloads of old automobile bodies. For years their gaping hulks grated harshly on the scenery of the surrounding valley. Time deals kindly with most things over the years, accordingly the ice of the Spring break-ups pounded the junk into the battered mass which we see today.

And so, the lot on the Don which first felt the impact of a pioneer's axe in 1832, may now gradually regain something of its birthright to sylvan beauty.

The lot on which the de Grassi house stands borders on the East Don river and is already graced with several century-old elms and other trees. The location can be described as outstanding. It lends itself to beautification. It is virtually the key to the east valley of the Don beyond the forks.

Since last November members of thbe Association have met there on Saturdays in an effort to renovate the dwelling and to clean up the lot, principally of the debris left in the wake of the Hurricane and flood of October 16th, 1954.

Since then, the dwelling has been raised and the floor levelled. Partitions were torn down to make one main room twenty-six by twenty-six, with kitchen adjoining. The plaster and old-fashioned hand-made laths were removed from the walls with the exception of one small section to be retained as an exhibit of pioneer construction. The place was rewired for electricity. Insulation to cover an area of fourteen hundred square feet was donated. A hardwood floor has been laid, and later a stone fireplace will grace the one large room. The new ceiling is of pine sheeting and the walls are of knotty pine. New widow frames have been made and new shingles cover the roof.

With the first days of Spring, volunteers will turn the lot into paths, shrub and flower borders and areas of flag stones. There will be benches and seats. A tiny brook which flows to the rear of the property will some day have its paddle wheel.

The Hurricane, so destructive, brought into being the possibility of this project, which will most certainly benefit conservation in the Don Valley. Its value to the Association and to its work will be immeasurable. The D.V.C.A. will have a place to meet, a place to set up exhibits of things of the outdoors, a headquarters for lectures, a meeting place for its hiking club, a haven where memebrs may enjoy relaxation in pleasant surroundings.

The Centre will become a show window for D.V.C.A. activities; it will identify the association and its work. The lot will be a stepping-off place for tours of the valley. The Centre will be seen by thousands of persons who pass it each day in motor cars. Over a period of time it will be known throughout the city and farther afield.

Phillipe de Grassi was born in Italy. His military career included service in both the French and British armies. He fought under Napoleon in Spain.

Winter 1955

Donlands Farm

DONLANDS FARM, when first opened up, stretched northwards on the east side of Don Mills Road from the present Hydro line to a point a few hundred feet south of Lawrence Ave. East. Along its entire length the farm ran easterly to Woodbine Ave. The farm also included an area west of Don Mills Road, where the International Business Machines, Barber Greene, Philco, Perfect Circle and other plants now stand.

This area was Crown land in 1850. It was opened for settlement by Taylor brothers in 1851, just over a century ago. The east half of lot one, concession 3, which is included in Donlands Farm, was secured from the Crown by George Taylor, through patent issued on June 17th, 1851. The picture on page 2 of "The Cardinal" June 15, 1952 issue, shows "stumping" operations on Donlands Farm.

Today, the farm and adjoining countryside is much as it was at the turn of the century. Proceeding northwards we observe on the left side of Don Mills Road the dwelling of Mr. Stan Fisher, the hydro lines, a market garden, the abandoned pioneer homestead of the Meagher family, and close to it the Meagher barn in good repair. Adjoining it a coke road leads to the residences of Mr. Kenneth McKenzie and of his son, Ian. North of this road farm fields stretched unbrokenly to the C.P.R. line until 1954. Last year a water main was laid across the east Don Valley from Scarboro, and in 1955 a wide strip of farmland was sacrificed for the Eglinton east extension.

Adjoining the extension near the edge of the Valley is the residence of Mrs. Murdock McKenzie. Across a field from it is a large barn and paddock.

On Don Mills Road, where the C.P.R. line crosses it, are to be seen the barns of the farm and a red brick dwelling. This dwelling was the original Taylor house of Donlands Farm. Several hundred yards east of Don Mills Road and secluded in a grove of trees, stood a stone house. It was destroyed by fire on January 29th, 1940. It was known as the Dillamore house. On November 16th, 1874, part of Donlands farm property was transferred to Mary Dillamore. Later the surname was Delomore. From the accounts of 'old timers' we can picture the farm in its original state as a solid belt of White pine. Mr. Robert Hunter, of Wexford, remembered when the bush adjoining Donlands Farm was a pinery. Four hundred acres of pine woods ran in a belt east from Don Mills Road along the present C.P.R. line to the fourth concession. According to Mr. Hunter some of the pine trees were six feet through and yielded fourteen cords of four foot cord wood, each cord measuring four feet by four by eight.

It would seem unbelievable to us today that such trees were used for cordwood. That they once existed is all too true. The hiker comes across their stumps in the woods of Donlands Farm; huge cavernous stumps which in my Boy Scout days served as hiding places during Scout games. Before felling these tree giants for lumber, it was necessary to lay a bed of saplings to break their fall and to prevent them from shattering into fragments from their own weight. White pine trees one hundred feet long and four and a half feet in diameter were common. When Taylor brothers first cleared Donlands Farm they cut down a White pine tree which yielded five thousand board feet of lumber and the tree was hollow twelve feet from the ground.

Mr. W.F.(Billy) Maclean, one time Federal Member of Parliament for York and proprietor of the 'Toronto World' took over part of Donlands Farm in 1904, gradually extending his holdings easterly to the Don River to include the Milne woollen mill property in the east valley of the Don near Lawrence Ave. His daughter Molly Maclean said: '*I think the property at that time comprised some nine hundred acres. Later he got what we still call the Martin field at the extreme south-east corner; the Dillamore farm and later the old 'Milne' woollen mill property joining Donlands in the valley to the north-east.*'

She said that at the time of the purchase there were two houses, one of which was the old red brick Taylor homestead right on the road south of the C.P.R. tracks. The other was a frame house which stood 'At the top of the hill north from the C.P.R. and lived in by the Smiths.' This dwelling was blown down in a gale in the year 1936.

Molly Maclean's remarks concerning Donlands Farm are summarized in this extract from one of her letters. It is particularly descriptive of the farm at the time of Maclean occupancy.

'At this time the entire west side of the farm was being rented by a Mr. Hariss for pasturing his beef cattle and I think this went on for some time after we took over as I distinctly remember real cow-boys in western get-ups, who boarded in the red brick house, and herded the cattle on ponies.'

'As well as these legitimate residences were two other unlisted ones. One was just a shack in the west bush, where lived a man of rather Gypsy appearance whose name I do no recall. Then in the east, or Maple bush, lived the Martin Brothers (bachelors) Arthur and Sam. They had squatter's rights, but these were not necessary with us as they were great favorites of ours and had an attractive little cottage and well-tended garden right on the river edge.'

'As far as I ever saw, everything they ate, used, or wore was carried down by hand, on foot. Though there were some old so-called Saw-mill roads to be seen, they had cut themselves steps in the hill from what my father later named Park Drive.'

'At this time our neighbours on the south were the Peddlers, who lived in the field stone house called the 'Dallimore house.''

'As my father wished to retain the red brick house to board farm men, he decided at once to build a fair-sized frame cottage to be lived in only in summer. This he hurried through as my mother had been very ill, and our Doctor had advised fresh air, sun and quiet.'

'Then ensued a series of most delightful summers and equally unpleasant winters spent in furnished houses in Toronto or Ottawa as the cottage was impossible to live in during the winter.'

'It stood on the hill overlooking the valley and Wexford, with the main line of the C.P.R. to Montreal on its north side. We had no trees very close but all around us were big luxurious Don Elms, Maples, etc. and in front below the house stood the most magnificent Basswood I have ever seen. Here we often had our afternoon tea.'

'We found ourselves gradually staying on later each Fall and years later after my mother died, my father and I decided to fix up the Dallimore house which we had now acquired and made it our year-round home. We added just as much again to the old stone house, trying hard to match the lovely work, using our field stone and getting old-time masons to do the work.'

'What country it was in those days, what perfect roads for the horse-minded, what rides and drives, solid sand from H.H.Taylor's corner (Don Mills Road and O'Connor Drive) over the 'Plains' to even the Woodbine Race Track. Big thorough-bred farms like Mr. Robert Davies Thorncliffe with its private race track, the very sporting Meagher family's or clan's thoroughbreds, which they both raced and hunted. Myself being driven to the 'Car' as we called it, meaning the head of

Broadview, where I was left off to join all the Davies and Taylor children for the street car ride to the Model school.'

'When my father still had the 'World' newspaper, Donlands became the motive for many very popular little editorials, the Sugar Bush, the natives of Wexford, Chris Stong the great Coon hunter, etc.'

In those days the Don Valley was quite unspoiled. Bridle trails leading to the Milne Mill were free of underbrush, and the valley flats free of weeds. Before the construction of railway the stream followed a natural course and flowed where it pleased.

A very small flag station named 'Valleydon' adjoined the C.P.R. near the Maclean cottage. 'The Natural History of the Toronto Region,' published in 1913, makes this reference to it. Under the heading 'Excursions' the book advises hikers 'to take Metropolitan line to Eglinton Ave., walk east two miles crossing the Don and continuing about one-half mile. More easily reached by taking th C.P.R. to Valleydon and walking south-west.' Mr. Maclean often took the C.P.R. to Valleydon after his day's work at the 'World'. A few steps across the meadow and this remarkable man was home; home to a world which filled his mind and his heart, for he loved Donlands Farm intensely. Up until 1944 a chimney and fireplace stood as the last mementos of the Maclean cottage. For many years in my memory of things this was the landmark of the area; a place to stop on a hike, or in which to find shelter during a summer storm. Today, only a pile of rubble remains to mark its memory. The iron which held it together had been taken away to serve some other purpose.

The surrounding fields, the distant woodlands, the pastures, despite the encroachment of factories and dwellings from the north and the west, are rural Ontario at its best; a scene to tug at one's heart strings, to make one hope and dream on a July day when the bobolinks sing in a frenzy of song, that it will never, never change.

There are several things I have long associated with Mrs. Murdock Mackenzie; the seclusion of the friendly acres surrounding her dwelling, an attractive cottage used by her and other members of the Fleming family; the woods just beyond her fence line carpeted in May with trilliums, and a ridge of land to the south of the cottage, which I am told is the shore of old Lake Iroquois.

The Eglinton extension has swept away the trail which led through the woods from Mrs. Mackenzie's residence to the east Don Valley. It was a trail cut through a grove of graceful beech trees. Throughout the year, they were a delight to the eye. In January their grey trunks blended with the snow in a portrait of nature at rest. May awakened the copper-coloured buds to new life. The solemn deep green foliage of July turned in October to the colour of deep brown. Some of the leaves remained on the trees throughout the Winter as so many pieces of flaxen paper.

The place I called Tanager Hollow, so remembered for the black and scarlet songsters which hid there and the thread of a brook, are gone

Fleming's Farm (Donlands) looking east from Don Mills Road, about where Ontario Science Centre is now situated. Ridge to left by barn is shoreline of old Lake Iroquois. Don Valley in background. Photo circa 1950.

The barns of Fleming's farm, July 24th, 1955. Scene looks south-east from C.P.R. tracks crossing Don Mills Road.

forever. Buried with them under the Eglinton extension, is the memory of many and many a hike. Beyond Tanager Hollow, stretched the slopes of the valley so restfully named Wild Flower Paradise, then the remnants of Maclean's sugar bush, where could be seen the foundations of the dwellings where the Martin brothers once lived, and almost alongside of it the vestiges of Maclean's maple sugar shanty.

Mrs. Mackenzie is the daughter of the late R.J.Fleming, who took over the farm in 1922. From this circumstance it was generally known as Fleming's Farm, a name familiar to all, and associated with the fine grey barns on Don Mills Road near the C.P.R. line. Herds of cattle still roam the pastures. The mechanical rhythm of farm machinery is heard out in the fields.

Here in the summer of 1955 stands the last fragment of rural Ontario to be seen in the immediate vicinity of Greater Toronto. Less than seven miles from Toronto City Hall it has retained the full measure of an unspoiled countryside, a place where the visitor may wander through the groves of deciduous trees planted by Mr. Maclean or down the valley slopes covered with thousands of Scots pines put there by him thirty years ago, or gaze at the massive trunks of the basswood tree, about which so many of his stories were written, or pause in the woods where succulent thimbleberries grow. The clay soil, the dense underbrush, the gushing spring, the wide broad farm fields, the site of the old sugar shanty, are things of a priceless heritage.

On a late August evening of this past summer I retraced the old familiar trails from Donlands Farm to the Don Valley once more. My path led me through maple woods to the headwaters of a little brook where at one time a beauty spot had been planned. The brook meandered through a meadow, lost itself in a tangle of cedars and bulrushes, a home for red-winged blackbirds in summer, and a shelter for a pair of long-eared owls in winter. I paused by the old sagging pioneer homestead of the Meaghers, where thirty-five years before Margaret Meagher had told me stories of the people who had once lived along the valley. I crossed a field now covered with birch trees but so covered in 1921 with puffballs as to be white with them. I came to the crest of the valley and walked down the logging road along which the timbers for the Meagher house and barn had been hauled, and where a man by the name of Burns had made charcoal and where a negro runaway slave had been chastised for misconduct. Then to the remnants of old orchards heavy with rosy fruit and nearby a fence of pine roots whose wood was rosy too.

All of this and much more belongs to another day, the days of Donlands and the Meagher farms, the days of picturesque scenery and picturesque people. In a decade most of it will be effaced forever.

Winter 1955

D.V.C.A. of East York Open House
September 11, 1955

If Phillipe de Grassi had been able to see the scene enacted in his homestead on September 11th, he would have marvelled indeed. His dwelling of a century ago, now one large room and kitchen finished in pine, was literally filled with people. A fire was blazing in a hearth where a few months before there had been no hearth. People milled about a fine old table where tea was poured for the occasion. Ladies passed biscuits around. Music was heard over a loud speaker and groups of people moved about the grounds, visiting the Conservation Centre and adjoining Art Centre.

What was back of all this? The event had been simply planned as an open house, an occasion on which members of the D.V.C.A. and dozens of other persons associated with conservation were given an opportunity to see what had been accomplished.

Most of them were already familiar with the story; how the house had been renovated following the ravages of Hurricane Hazel, and how the surrounding area had been cleared of chicken coops, piles of junk, and turned into some semblance of a beauty spot.

A word of mention here for those who helped to plan and make the open house a success. Miss Anne McMillan headed up the planning for decorations, placing of wild flowers in the room, etc. Miss Vera Clarke assisted by Misses Austin and Shirley Montague arranged for the cookies. Mel Andrews made the signs and secured the cream. Bob Speakman organized the Scout parking patrol. Mr. J. Giguere supervised the parking. Mr. Dennis Ince provided the music over a loud speaker and used his equipment for the purpose. Irene Meyer helped Anne McMillan. Tea pourers were Mrs. Percy Black, Mrs. Chas. Sauriol, Mrs. Stan. Fisher, Mrs. T. Simpson. Mrs. Marguerite Edwards was hostess. Alf Ainsworth organized the police patrol of Don Mills Road. Reception committee consisted of Alf Ainsworth, Chas. Corey, J.D.Thomas, Norman McKay, John Stevenson, Hank Loriaux. Ken Moore entered new memberships and disposed of Cardinal badges. Stan Fisher handled newspaper publicity. Visitors included Roads' Commissioner All, Lex Schrag (Globe & Mail), Anne Merrill (Globe & Mail), Herb Richardson, Chief Conservation Engineer; Eric Baker of Humber Conservation Authority; Charles Clifford of Don Valley Conservation Authority; Ald. Donald Summerville; H.Stanley Honsberger, Chairman of Don Valley Conservation Authority; Murdock McIver, Secretary of Don Valley Conservation Authority; Mr. T.C.Main of 'Ducks Unlimited'; Jack Allan of Sunnybrook Nurseries; Mrs. E.D.Waterson.

Winter 1955

The Don Valley Nature Study Club of 1900

'Two trees loaded with honey taken within a fortnight in a Canadian January seven miles from the City Hall of Toronto with its 300,000 population, is it not something of a marvel? Only the beautiful valley of the Don could furnish it.'

This quotation is from the 'Toronto World' of January 1907. It describes one of the activities of the Don Valley Nature Study Club; a nature study group which roamed the valley at the turn of the century and later. The guiding star of the club was W.F.(Billy)Maclean, then owner of Donlands Farm. His acres were at the disposal of the club as were also the columns of the 'Sunday World' Supplement. Long before Anne Merrill, Hugh Halliday or Jim Baillie delighted Toronto readers with stories of nature, the 'World' was doing good work in this field. The late Owen Staples published his own impressions of the Don Valley in the 'Telegram'. Macpherson Ross also wrote on the Don Valley for that same newspaper.

The Don Valley Nature Study Club drew its membership from local residents; people who lived on farms now part of Wexford's sub-divisions. They were hardy outdoor folk who knew the valley, lived near it, and roamed in it throughout the seasons.

It is not surprising that their experiences were varied and colourful. Nor is it surprising that W.F.Maclean, an enterprising newspaper man, should see the value of their homespun adventures as features for his newspaper.

The group took nature study seriously. The appearance of a blackbird during a spring-like January, or a sudden flooding of the Don were occasions of great discussion.

On a mild January Sunday (1907) the group stood on the edge of the valley near the present C.P.R. bridge arguing over an important event: Chris Stong, from Woodbridge, the 'greatest coon hunter of all time' had invaded the Wilson flats, and right under the nose of the club he had found a bee tree loaded with honey. The club could not rest easy until it had shown its ability to do likewise.

The opportunity came on the January day already referred to. The temperature had risen to 60 degrees, causing a premature break-up of the river ice. A huge basswood stood in the flats of thbe East Don Valley on the west side of the river below the C.P.R. high level bridge. The story is told in the words of one of the members: 'In a few minutes the tree was down. It was a shell. It broke near the bee's quarters. They came out in thousands. A club member filled one of the big pails with the finest pure clover comb honey in a few seconds. Not less than a hundred pounds of honey was in the tree.'

'It is many a day since over a hundred pounds of honey was taken out of a bee tree in the third week of January when the temperature was above 60 degrees and the river running a great flood through the flats. The bee tree reached the flood with its top when it came down.'

Then he observes that such an event could only take place in the Don Valley.

Chris Stong (see 'The Cardinal', Fall 1952 issue for the full story) sought out wild honey as he did coons. He often took out two hundred pounds of fine comb honey from a single tree. And he took the honey as he did the coons, without cutting down the tree. He did not consider Winter as a good time to take honey.

Harvey Armstrong, also a member of the Club, ran a trap line through the valley. He invented a special trap for catching mink.

Many seasons have come and gone since the Don Valley Nature Study Club carried on its activities in the Don Valley. I remember one of the members (then an old man) telling me that they had lived quiet, happy lives in the Valley, making their living from the rich farm land on which it bordered and finding their entertainment in the variations of the seasons.

Today other nature and hiking clubs roam the Valley, living with the seasons in their own way and enjoying what the Valley still presents to them in all of its facets.

Flood Damage in the Don Valley

The Aftermath

It was only on Saturday morning that I was able to see the full impact of the flood waters. The Forks of the Don appeared a devastated area, water-soaked and mud-laden. As mentioned, the Don Mills Road had been under some five feet of water. The Don Valley Art people had just finished an extension of their clubhouse. Water had risen to about half of the height of the building. The interior was partly ruined. Oil paintings were found embedded in mud; carpets were soaked with it. The lawns and all the surroundings were buried under a covering of muddy sand.

On the road motor cars stalled by the storm showed evidence of having been covered with the mud-laden water. Also along the road were to be seen sagging telephone and hydro poles, branches, tree-trunks, and soupy mud. The cottage adjoining the Art Centre had also been flooded, and the furnishings ruined.

A cable bridge which I used to cross the Don, and which had survived many years of ordinary floods, had been battered and torn from its moorings. An area of garden land, a few days before covered with clover and raspberry canes, was buried beneath several feet of silt. It was a scene to make one feel sick at heart.

There seemed to be no end to the destruction. Elsewhere sections of Don Mills Road had been gouged out. Todmorden Park had been under flood. In the Pottery Road area, two bridges had been partly washed out, and Whitewood's Riding School had become a miniature sea of mud.

Further up the valley the destruction took place in the form of caved-in banks, ripped-out hillsides, toppled trees, washed-out bridges.

I had read many times the accounts of the floods of April 4, 1850, and of September 14, 1878, and the details of the terrible damage they brought about; but I doubt if these floods could compare with the city-wide disaster of the 15th and 16th of October, 1954.

The Great Rainstorm of September, 1878 was not to be compared in destructive powers with Hurricane Hazel of October 15th, 1954.

Sunday in the Valley

Further visits to the Don Valley on Sunday produced evidence of more destruction. The C.N.R. line was washed out in many places. Crews and equipment were busily engaged putting the line back into service. The flood waters had undermined the embankments in other places, and these huge, gaping holes had to be filled in.

On the lower Don, near Rosedale Ravine, the apiary of John McArthur was washed away. Bee-hives could be seen floating about on the flats half a mile from their original location. Elsewhere residents were trying to salvage what they could of water-soaked belongings.

The Clay Banks

Perhaps one of the most significant indications of the fury of the flood was to be seen at the 'Clay Banks' swimming hole on the East Don. Now it could not be more appropriately named, for the flood waters had sheared off the top of a triangle of land 50 x 75 ft. Six feet of topsoil disappeared, leaving exposed a bed of clay and a layer of heavy gravel, laid down perhaps thousands of years ago.

Not in our time, or perhaps at any time, will this clay be covered over. From the clay a tiny spring which had spent centuries in solitude now flowed for the first time in the light of day. On the opposite shore, fresh deposits of gravel had been left in the wake of the storm.

The ravages of the flood are seen in the number of bridges, side cut, washed out, or otherwise battered by the storm. Every bridge on the Don suffered some damage. Some were huge structures, others were of iron frame work, others of wood, and a few like my own were cable foot bridges. The bridge over the Don leading to Toronto Brick Works was side cut. It was quickly put back into use by the Company. Pottery Road bridge was side cut. A huge gaping hole had to be filled on its southern approach. The iron bridge with plank floor over the east Don in Milne's hollow was also side cut. The bridge spanning the east Don on York Mills Road east of Bayview was closed following the storm. Some of the railway bridges were also side cut by the flood waters.

The 'before' and 'after' pictures of beautiful Patterson pond on Don Head Farms near Richmond Hill is a tragic portrayal of the ruin of one of the loveliest beauty spots on the Don.

To have seen the waters in their full fury early Saturday morning October 16th was indeed an unforgettable sight. Jim Wooler, a rural postman living on the Don Mills Road near the forks, spent most of the night on the alert. At three A.M. as he stood on the Don Mills Road, the moon came out from behind the clouds and cast a feeble light on an awesome scene; most of the valley floor was a surging tide of muddy water. The quiet of the night was shaken by the reverberations of huge floating trees pounding the buttresses of the bridge at the forks. The water was littered with fast-moving objects, not discernible in the darkness. Lower down the valley other persons watched the water rise higher and higher as the railway tracks were covered, then the approaches to the brick works. Sounds of muffled explosions came from the brick kilns as the water reached the fires in the kilns and extinguished them; a strange note in a scene of desolation.

Golf courses could be added to the list of damaged bridges. Most of the courses ranged over land watered by rivers or creeks and all of them had small bridges. The courses were heavily covered with silt or gravel, and the debris of piled-up trees, branches, litter. In the Thornhill district all bridges of the three neighbouring clubs were washed out, also at Thornhill a landslide washed out the manager's house at the 18th green.

Rosedale Club sustained damaged to the amount of $40,000. Mel Andrews, D.V.C.A member, has estimated that the East Don at peak flood level was one hundred times greater than its normal October flow.

Throughout the valley the ribs of sand and the bleached accumulations of silt, bring to mind some giant rotting carcass. The odor of decay is brought faintly from the lowlands where muddy slime lies several feet deep.

A dwelling stands abandoned, door swung out, windows open, debris littered about on the veranda. In the kitchen the unwashed dishes, still in the sink, tell of a departure in panic when the storm struck on Friday. Along the fringe of the valley, the gaily-painted leaves of Fall seem in utter contradiction to the scenes of destruction closer to the river shore.

But already peope are busy setting things in order. Railway crews are filling the gaping holes in the roadbed. Furniture, mattresses, and belongings are set to dry, or abandoned if beyond recovery. Bridge crews, road crews and highway crews are scattered along the roads. Perhaps in some gardens the added layer of washed-out top-soil will prove to be in the years to come a benefit. Kiwanis members make their rounds, visiting stricken families offering help of food, clothing, money.

Perhaps we have learned a lesson. There were rumours of housing developments on the flats of the upper valley. Today, such projects are buried with the flood, or should be. We wonder who would dare, in the face of Toronto's most appalling loss of life, to suggest that river flats could be now used for building purposes.

The first significant reactions to the flood are beginning to appear in the news. Fred G.Gardiner, Chairman Metropolitan Toronto Council, has stated: *'We must be more insistent that sub-dividers must not be allowed to develop lands lying next to rivers. They must be zoned as green belts and taken over by Metro or by local municipalities.'*

Reeves of several of the municipalities are making haste to ask that flood sites be acquired as parks. Action will be taken to prevent building in the river plots.

One need merely glance at the combined photo and sketch of Raymore Drive (Toronto Star, Oct. 18) to observe how perilously close this washed-out street was to the Humber River.

Loss of Life

The loss of life during the flood is by far the greatest loss. The loss of property is no small consideration, and the loss of soil by millions of tons is a permanent one to the country. A river of rainwater in the middle of farm fields—a river of sufficient size to derail a train—is an indiscretion for which we are going to pay in terms of much-needed soil.

We know there has been an almost utter disregard for the basic requirements of conservation in sections of the flood area. We have sheared off the topsoil of farmlands and sold it, leaving the fields in a condition somewhat comparable to a scalped head.

We have turned our storm-sewer pipes into our ravines; our pumping stations have also emptied their contents into those ravines. We have drained the water from our streets by letting that water pour over valley slopes. We have literally made of these valleys a drain board through which torrents of water could too easily escape.

The Ultimate Story

Does it not seem reasonable to suggest, in view of the millions of dollars of property damage which has occurred, that every effort should be made to be prepared for future flood emergencies? Does not this loss point to the need for conservation?

We should not rest until we have planted and protected the entrance and sides of every gully; until we have put back the cover on every piece of land which should be covered, and can be covered, until we have taken reasonable steps to prevent the quick run-off of water, so that it will not raise the level of our rivers by three and four feet within twenty minutes, ending in floods such as occurred last week. We should make our river valleys as safe from flash floods as humanly possible.

Summer 1955

The Fight for Rosedale Ravine

AS ONE CROSSES PRINCE EDWARD VIADUCT at the intersection of Parliament street and Bloor street and glances to the north, there appears a long wooded ravine containing hardwoods principally, and the stiff broom-like foliage of an occasional White pine.

Historically the creek (now covered over) was known as the Brewer's creek. Through his writings, naturalist Ernest Thompson Seton made this ravine known the world over.

The ravine is actually the Castle Frank ravine and Rosedale ravine lies to the north of it. Eye-leasing in any season, it drew no particular attention or evoked any special appreciation other than the fact that it was there. It was considered part of the Green Belt which slumbered in the security of the protection which Green Belts enjoyed—so the public thought.

Early in February 1955, a resident of the area sounded a first unbelievable note of alarm. A firm of Montreal promotors had purchased land adjoining the ravine and were preparing to erect an immense apartment building with a rear descent of some 125 feet into the wall of the ravine. The plan consisted of a split-level building, with three storeys on the table land, but running the length of nine storeys into the ravine. To put the matter simply, it was found that the city by-law, while limiting the height of apartment buildings up to 35 feet on the table land, made no specific mention of descent into the ravine. This loophole gave unlimited scope to the promoters and they made the best of it.

Ravine lands had been considered of no property value; everyone familiar with Toronto's Green Belt plans respected them. With the introduction of this new apartment plan however, they became of great land value, as evidenced by the fact that a price of $220,000 was paid for the five and a half acres of land on which the apartment building was to be erected. Other apartment buildings could be thus anchored to ravine walls until the Green Belt would become a canyon of brick, stone and windows.

It will be seen that the promoters of the plan were acting most astutely. For twenty-five years conservationists had been fighting for the preservation of Rosedale and other ravines; now an apartment builder could benefit from this effort, set his apartment down into the wall of the ravine still surrounded by trees with a fine southern exposure looking towards Bloor street, where it would be quite impossible to erect a building across from it.

Shortly after Mrs. Margaret Scrivener had sounded off the alarm, the Don

Valley Authority passed a resolution to have the land expropriated. The 'Save the Ravines' advocates mustered their strength, called meetings and won support at the level of local groups of which the D.V.C.A. was one. The three newspapers gave the campaign full publicity, both in reporting, cartoons, and editorials.

On February 21st, 1955, Mrs. Scrivener described the beauty of the ravine to members of her local Home and School Club, and les than twelve hours later a crew of men appeared in the ravine and proceeded to cut down many of the trees. The move was an unfortunate one for them, because it gave 'The Save the Ravines' committee strength when it met the Mayor and Board of Control on February 23rd. After a fair presentation the committee obtained consent to have the land expropriated. The tree cutting was stopped.

Later in the day, however, after listening to a representation from the opposing side, the Mayor and Board of Control suspended their original motion of expropriation pending a second appearance to be arranged for Monday, February 28th, at which delegates from 'The Save the Ravines' group and representatives of Kensington Industries would be present. At the meeting Mrs. Scrivener retained Donald Fleming, M.P. (P.C.) Eglinton as counsel, and myself as spokesman for the Don Valley Conservation Association.

Twenty-one letters from conservation and ratepayers groups assuring Mr. Fleming of their support were read. Each group represented several thousands of citizens. Mr. Fleming foresaw that a precedent would be established which would be followed by other builders. I stressed the irreplaceable value of all ravines, and elaborated on the point that we did not know as yet what their future value would be in the form of wildwood and wild life sanctuaries.

James Crang, the project architect, and Norman Bell of Kensington Industries produced sketches of the apartments, enhancing the factor of landscaping.

Controller Cornish, after an outline of basic points, cast his vote in favor of expropriation. He was followed by Controller Belyea, who said that expropriation would stop further exploitation of ravine lands. Controller Brand cast his vote against expropriation. Controller Balfour voted along with Controllers Belyea and Cornish. Mayor Phillips also voted for expropriation, which made the vote four to one in favor.

On the same day, February 28th, the Mayor and Board of Control met with Council at 2 p.m. The meeting lasted until 5 a.m. Tuesday morning and City Council finally voted to expropriate the Rosedale ravine site at a cost of $400,000. The vote was 13 to 6.

On March 9th, 1955, Metro Council approved the debentures to cover the cost of expropriation with a majority vote of 14 to 5.

On March 18th the expropriation move brought a strong protest from Labor Council. On March 19th apartment builders organized to fight the so-called 'pressure groups'. On March 21st Mayor Phillips in a public address said: 'we must not sacrifice parklands or beauty spots or destroy the character of neighbourhoods.'

On March 23rd Board of Control decided to keep the door open to apartment builders who had filed plans before Council voted to change the by-law. The only exception was that of proposed apartment construction in Rosedale ravine. In reply to this decision Ratepayers Associations called a protest meeting on March 26th and passed a resolution to ask City Council to suspend issuance of all apartment buiding permits pending a general review of the zoning by-law as it applied to erection of apartment houses in residential areas. On this occasion J.D.Thomas was spokesman for the D.V.C.A.

On the following Monday application for apartment buildings planned under the old regulations were rejected by City Council at a hectic six-hour Council meeting.

On March 29th the Municipal Board heard both sides of the 'Save the Ravine' story. The Chairman criticized City Council's indifference over the acquisition of Green Belt lands in the past.

The Board announced that its decision regarding the Rosedale ravine would be made later in the week.

On April 4th, 1955, the Ontario Municipal Board granted the city permission to expropriate the controversial five and a half acre parcel on Rosedale ravine, thus blocking the building of a multi-million dollar apartment planned for erection at Dale and McKenzie avenues.

Summer 1955

The Don Improvement

ALMOST EVERYONE LIVING IN THE GREATER TORONTO AREA is familiar with the view of the Don River as it flows sluggishly below the bridges at Eastern Ave., Queen, Dundas and Gerrard Streets. This scene is readily identified with the view of decaying palisades which stretch along each bank of the river in an almost continuous line from Eastern Avenue or thereabouts to the Bloor Street (Prince Edward viaduct).

Here and there the piles, as they are called, have been removed or may have rotted away. In other places the tops of the logs only are showing because of the silt left in the wake of many spring freshets. Near Bloor Street the stream has broken away from the piles and has traced a new course for itself.

From the Queen Street bridge an opening in the palisade on the west bank is observed. It was used to pull small craft out of the water to the river shore. Looking from the bridge northwards, the visitor sees a view perhaps unique in Canada: the waters of the lower Don move slowly past the palisades over which bend long rows of graceful willows. The arches of three bridges bind the foliage of one river bank with that of the other.

Few persons suspect today that a generation ago the lower Don was a major topic of discussion. Over the stream hovered the dreams of men who saw great things in store for it. Thousands of citizens were divided in opinion as to the practicability of those dreams.

Early in the 80's the Don pursued a meandering course down the lower Don valley, and particularly so from Bloor Street to the bay. Here it flowed through weedy marshes, comparable to those which we see at the mouth of the Rouge, the Credit and the Humber rivers. The course of the meandering stream was shown in the maps of the time, but perhaps most effectively in the map reproduced on page 5 of this issue. Gradually there emerged a plan to straighten the Don. It is said the assassination of President Garfield in 1881 made it necessary for Mayor McMurrick of Toronto and the city clerk to be in Cleveland to attend the funeral.

While in Cleveland, the Mayor observed the manner in which the Cuyahoga river had been compelled to flow where it would be of most use to industry. He felt that the Don could be dealt with similarly. The Mayor and other civic representatives had been interested in the project of Mr. Alderman Davies to straighten the winding course of the lower Don.

In the meantime, Alderman Davies, who doubted whether Council would back up his project, organized a company to obtain the land, reclaim it and lease it to manufacturers.

In the 'Globe' of January 8th, 1881, there appeared an item which to all intents coincided with the plans of Alderman Davies. It read: 'Proposed to form a company to render the Don navigable for large craft. The project of improving and utilizing the River Don, which has engaged attention of one or two individuals at various times, bids fair to take a practicable shape.'

A printed circular, from which an extract is copied here, was addressed to the land owners on both banks of the river. It read: 'A few gentlemen are willing to form themselves into a company for the purpose of widening, straightening, deepening and otherwise improving the River Don, so as to allow vessels drawing fourteen feet of water entering and navigating the same, but will not proceed in the matter until some satisfactory arrangements are made, giving them the right to purchase all the land they require for the purpose, and with that view have requested me to confer with yourself, and others owning the land on each side of the river.' There was no record of a signature.

During the years immediately following the appearance of this notice the subject of the straightening of the Don was discussed many times. Many persons felt that by straightening the course of the stream a valuable industrial property would be made available in place of the then existing marshland in the heart of the city.

But there was still another reason for straightening the Don, and some knowledge of it is gained in a letter which Mr. W.V.Van Horne, President of the Canadian Pacific Railway Co., wrote to the Mayor of Toronto, under date of January 23, 1890. It read in part: 'Early in 1885, or nearly five years ago, the Canadian Pacific Railway Co. took definite steps towards securing an independent entrance to Toronto... The plans and operations of the company were frequently discussed with the Mayor, the City Engineer, and different members of the City Council, and the utmost publicity was given to them in the city press, as early as May, 1886 with elaborate engravings...

'In April, 1888, an agreement was brought about between the Grand Trunk and the Canadian Pacific companies that seemed to remove the only obstruction in the way of the realization of the plans of the latter.'

'In a report addressed to Mr. MacMillan, President of the Council, dated June 21, 1889, the city engineer says: *It is doubtless familiar to you that when the Don Improvement was first projected provision was made on either bank merely for sidings or switching tracks for railways as well as roads and streets. It was intended apparently, that a siding and switching track should be placed next to the river, and between the river and the street, that would serve both vessels using the Don and wagons using the street and storehouse abutting thereon, etc.'* 'Many months have elapsed and the work remains at a standstill.'

The straightening of the Don was therefore considered necessary to provide land primarily for industrial purposes, and to also make available an additional railway entrance to Toronto. The Don with a greater depth of water after improvement could also be used to convey shipping up to the Queen Street station.

On a Saturday afternoon in September 1886, the people of Toronto went to the polls and voted on an issue 'to improve and straighten the river Don so as to secure the sanitary condition of that part of the City of Toronto contiguous to the said river.'

'Statutes, By-Laws and Documents' relating to the straightening and improvement of the River Don (compiled by Thomas Caswell and published in 1889) covers all of the details of the project.

From then on, the lower Don river and lower valley of the Don lost their original appearance. Gone the small five islands in the stream between Queen and Winchester streets; gone the care-free ice skating on the river; the boating to picnic spots upstream. With 'the Don Improvement', the last vestiges of a sylvan lower Don Valley disappeared forever.

The contract for 'the Don Improvement' called for the excavation and dredging of a channel from the Winchester street bridge to the south side of the bar dividing Ashbridge's Bay in the Toronto marsh from the waters of the lake, at a depth of 14 feet below 'zero' level of the lake.

The channel was to be 'piled' on both sides. The Gerrard and Eastern Avenue bridges were to be removed and new bridges constructed in their place. Additional 'fill' required for the job was to be taken from the side hills adjoining the Don valley, which when removed greatly altered the appearance of the landscape from Queen to Winchester streets.

The specifications for the wood to be used on the job were such as to make a present day builder's mouth water. For example: 'the piles shall be cedar, sound and straight and free from all projecting knots, 30 feet long and 10 inches across at the small end. Rock elm (now rare) pieces 12 by 9 inches shall be provided on both sides of the piles. The timber to be used in bends and bridges shall consist of good, sound White pine, having a clear straight grain, and free from sapwood, loose or dead knots, waves and other symptoms of decay. The timber used in upper cords, end trusses, and compression braces shall be of the best quality of White pine free from all defects. Floor beams shall be White oak of good and approved quality.' From these specifications it would seem that good timber was still plentiful in 1888.

The contract was secured by Messrs. Manning and MacDonald on the understanding that they would finish 'the whole of the above works by 1st day of November, 1888.

The estimated cost of 'the Don Improvement', including the cost of expropriated lands, was $300,000.00. My father worked on 'the Don Improvement' and operated a dredge for the firm of Manning and MacDonald.

The newly-made 'the Don Improvement' soon became the cause of a lively dispute between the Grand Trunk and Canadian Pacific Railway companies. Both claimed right-of-way over this newly-formed access to Toronto. A long, bitter fight ensued, with Major E.D.'Ned' Clarke bearing the brunt of the battle. 'Everyone interested seemed to place a different interpretation on 'the Don Improvement' act, and when one railway endeavoured to cross its line over the other, legal rights and tempers flared. Barricades were erected, loads of ballast were deliberately dumped and, finally, even construction crews fell into pitched battle. It provided plenty of excitement for the populace at large, who flocked to the scene in large numbers to witness the struggle and to take sides. Eventually the case went to the Privy Council, where it was ruled that the C.P.R. should cross the river at Winchester street to the east side, and the Grand Trunk extend its right-of-way up the west bank.'

Extracts from the correspondence of the time emphasize the situation. On December 28th, 1888, Major Clarke had stated in a letter to Mr.C. Sprout, the City Engineer, that there was no dispute about the C.P.R. coming down the Don Improvement, 'but why was the company allowed to select the most favourable part of the Improvement, and to occupy it exclusively to the detriment of other railway companies.'

On February 15th, 1889, Mr.R.M.Wells of the C.P.R. said that his company had never dreamed of occupying this reserve without the consent of the City, or without making full and fair compensation for it. To which the

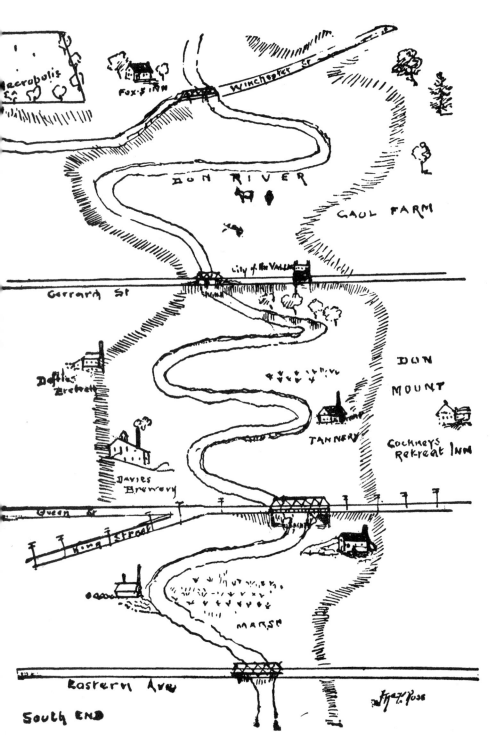

Major replied on February 23rd, stating that *'section 9 of the Act expressly provides that all railways shall be entitled to the use of the Improvement on equal terms.' 'Am I to understand that it is now claimed on behalf of the* C.P.R. *that they have a right to appropriate an absolute estate in the property which has been taken and improved by the City under the 'Don Improvement Act.'*

On February 25th Major E.F.Clarke wrote a letter to the Council in which he said: *'The Canadian Pacific Railway Company state for the proper conduct of their business they should have exclusive use of at least two tracks on the Improvement, while the Grand Trunk Railway Company points out that the plans under which the work is being carried out do not comply with the requirements of the Act.'* J.D.Edgar, Esq., Belt Line Railway Company, asked Major Clarke *'how the proposed location of the* C.P.R. *will effect the bringing of the proposed Belt Line Railway into the city by way of the Don Improvement.'*

And in conclusion, this extract from Mr. Well's reply of February 25th, 1889, to Major Clarke: *'Surely'* he says, *'it was not contemplated that the main lines of the* C.P.R. *or any other company, entering a city like Toronto, should be over and upon a couple of sidings. If this is the only route by which the* C.P.R. *can enter Toronto from the east, the company would save time and money by abandoning the Don branch altogether, travelling five and half miles further and enter as it now does via West Toronto junction,'* etc.

Mr. Wells then quoted a telegram which he 'dispatched' on September 30th, 1886, to Mr. Van Horne following a meeting with Mayor Howland. *'Had meeting with Mayor Howland, the City Engineer in favour of strip along river bank 23 feet wide for unloading and general purposes, then strip 26 feet for use in common for railways, then 26 feet exclusively for Canadian Pacific, then 50 feet for street, then 200 feet for lots.'* Wells concluded with this statement: *'The company neither asks for nor desires an inch of land or a single privilege from the city except upon the ordinary business principle of paying full and fair value for them.'*

Today C.P.R. locomotives and diesels pull Montreal and Ottawa passenger trains along 'the Don Improvement', crossing the Don at Winchester street, then along the east side of the valley, then crossing it via the high-level 'half-mile' bridge. Along the same route of 'the Don Improvement', locomotives and diesels, the pride of the C.N.R. pull other passenger trains up the east Don valley on a line eventually leading to North Bay, other Northern Ontario points and to Winnipeg.

Don Valley Conservation Association train trips over both of these lines have given thousands of conservationist-excursionists an opportunity to observe the languid sluggish stream and the decaying piles as we best know them. Nor did these excursionists suspect that in this stream one man saw the potentialities of a great artery of trade: *'Howland's Folly'* the dream was called, but that is a story for another day.

The Don Valley Brick Works

DOMINATING THAT SECTION OF THE DON VALLEY which lies immediately to the north of Prince Edward viaduct is to be seen a huge excavation. From the ramp of the viaduct, the walls of this clay pit bear some resemblance to Scarboro bluffs.

As the visitor walks along the C.N.R. tracks past Rosedale ravine, then along the remnants of the roadbed of the 'old' Belt Line Railway, he becomes aware of the true size of the main pit. Standing on its brink, he appraises its depth at perhaps one hundred feet and extending five hundred feet from end to end. On the north side, the original valley mount, rises in a series of shelves for another fifty feet above the pit and extends for a considerable distance northwards. From the brink of this man-made precipice a steam shovel sprawls turtle-like at the bottom of the pit. It seems as a child's toy.

Adjoining the pit along its southern and eastern boundaries are to be seen numerous brick kilns, sheds, piles of brick and slabs of shale. Four towering chimneys dominate the property. On each chimney a word is lettered, making up the name 'Don-Valley-Brick-Works'.

In the Spring of the year 1882, the area was dotted with meadows and the valley walls were covered with trees. It sheltered the ravine which Ernest Thompson Seton dramatized in his book 'Two Little Savages', a book which was based in part on his adventures in the Don Valley.

In the month of April of that year, Mr.Wm.T.Taylor, and a helper, were at work erecting a fence. Mr. Taylor paused from time to time to examine the cores of the clay brought to the surface from the post holes which he had dug. He thought the clay was of unusually fine texture. He became curious as to its possibilities for brick making. The next day, he returned to the site bringing with him two small cigar boxes which he packed with clay. He sauntered down the valley to a small brick works then in operation in the vicinity of the Bloor street viaduct. A lively discussion as to the quality of the clay ensued between Mr. Taylor and the proprietor of the brick works. Here is a record of their conversation as told to me by a descendant of the Taylor family. Said Mr. Taylor: 'These samples will bake red.' To which the other man replied: 'They certainly will not, that's ordinary brick clay and they'll bake grey.'

A few days later Mr. Taylor returned to the kiln and according to the story his sample bricks had baked cherry red. The proprietor admitted that the bricks were two of the best samples he had ever seen, and 'if the entire seam was like the samples,' he said, 'Mr. Taylor had a gold mine in clay lying in that bend of the Don Valley.'

William Taylor told his brothers John and George of the 'find', whereupon the three brothers decided after considerable testing of the clay seam to establish their own brick manufacturing plant in the Don Valley. The enterprise became known as the Don Valley Pressed Brick Works.

Taylor Brothers were described in the catalogues of their day as manufacturers of fine grade pressed brick in all colours and designs, also of fire-clay, fire-bricks, sewer pipes, etc. The 'etc.' included ornamental Terra Cotta, a product popular enough in its day to merit a catalogue of its own. Several of Toronto's older buildings are decorated with ornamental Terra Cotta produced by Taylor Brothers in their Don Valley plant.

A gold medal was awarded to Taylor Brothers for their exhibit at the Toronto Industrial Fair of 1894. The firm also won several world fair medals.

Taylor Brothers produced twelve million bricks a year. The firm carried on a large export trade with the United States.

Robert Davies acquired the Don Valley Brick Works in 1901, retaining ownership until 1928.

As these lines are written (Summer 1955) bricks are still produced from the clay of the original Taylor pit, which is expanding from day to day. High up on the ledges above the pit, steam shovels are removing fresh 'overburden'; an operation which precedes the enlarging of the quarry. Areas of the surrounding Don Valley flats have been filled and levelled with this 'top stuff'. Shale secured from the excavations can be used for the making of walks, garden paths. It is sold for these and other purposes.

Under date of December 30th, 1944, the third annual report of the City of Toronto Planning Board makes this mention of the quarry: 'The Don Valley Brick Works is included in the belt (Greenbelt) on the assumption that, as time goes on, the exhaustion of clay deposits will make this site available.' One might ask: Available for what? It would take fifty years to fill the pit.

Wm.T.Taylor died on January 3rd, 1944, at the age of 86. He spent his last days at Bellehaven, 1068 Broadview Ave., the residence which he built in 1887. Under his eyes to the last were the chimneys of the industry which he had founded.

Wm.Lea, founder of Leaside, recorded the fact that Helliwell and Eastwood made brick on the Don in 1820, using bricks for the construction of a brewery and distillery.

Before that date (November 24th, 1796) the Honorable Peter Russell wrote to Governor Simcoe declaring that 'the bricks Mr. McGill had made at York were so ignorantly done that none of them could be used.

The Players manufactured brick near the north-west corner of Danforth and Broadview Avenues. These were described as 'wire bricks'. Small quarries were also established off Pottery Road at the foot of Beechwood Drive.

In the year 1908, Wm.T.Taylor founded the Sun Brick Co. on lot 11, concession three East York. Within a few years of the founding of the Sun Brick Co., Wm.Taylor disposed of his interests to Sir Henry Pellett, builder of Casa Loma. I remember the Sun Brick quarry as a water-filled pond or small lake, large enough to provide rowing and swimming for numerous youngsters and deep enough to drown several of them. About 1938, dumping operations were started and today the Sun Brick quarry which lay in the valley near Beechwood Drive is a landmark of the past.

The land on which the quarry was located was purchased in 1954 by the Municipality of East York. It is proposed to make a park of it. The park could suitably be called Terry's Field. There is evidence that it was owned originally by Parshall Terry, a sergeant in Butler's Rangers and early pioneer of the Don. In his notes William Lea makes this reference to Terry's field: 'The clearing he made in a high part of the flats in a large bend of the hill is still called Terry's field. (Lot 11, concession three). Eastwood and Skinner moved his house and rebuilt it at the Don Mills, where it remains to this day on the estate of the late Thos.Taylor.' NOTE: *The dwelling is still standing near Pottery Road. Mr. Lea refers to Terry's mill as the new saw mill. It was closed down about 1820.*

Fall 1955

The Exploit of Charlotte and Cornelia de Grassi

THE STORY OF CAPTAIN PHILLIPE DE GRASSI has already been related in the December 15th, 1953, issue of The Cardinal. It was there stated that Captain de Grassi drew a grant of two hundred acres near the forks of the Don, where he endured the hardships of a settler in a new country. He wrote: 'After the fire, I managed amidst great trials and difficulties to struggle on until that unfortunate rebellion broke out in 1837, when Mr.W.L.Mackenzie thought to take upon himself more than regal functions and declared that my property with that of many other loyal men, should be parcelled out among his followers.'

On the evening of the day on which the rebellion broke out, (Dec. 4th, 1837), de Grassi went to Toronto to offer his services to the Government. He was accompanied by his two daughters, Charlotte and Cornelia. These three narrowly escaped being taken prisoners by Mathews troop which was going to Helliwell's place. This information implies that de Grassi followed a trail leading from the forks of the Don to the lower valley, near Pottery Road. In Toronto he found excitement and confusion everywhere. At the Government House he joined the Scarboro militia forces under Col. McLean.

While at the Parliament House, he said he would endeavour to ascertain the number of rebels on Yonge Street. He related this incident as follows: *'One of my daughters, about thirteen years of age, accordingly who was a capital rider, rode out under pretense of wishing to know the price of a sleigh, went to the Wheelwright's shop close to Montgomery's tavern, and being suspected was taken prisoner by some of the rebels who ordered her to dismount.'* During the scuffle which followed, Mackenzie came out with the news that the Western Mail had been taken. Profiting from the general excitement the de Grassi girl had the presence of mind to ride off at full speed. Several muskets were discharged at her. A ball went through her saddle and another grazed her clothing. *'Arrived back in Toronto,'* Captain de Grassi relates, *'she was taken before Sir F.B.Head, the Governor, to whom she gave valuable information as to the number and condition of the rebels—thus the Loyalists were encouraged, measures were taken to meet Mackenzie's attack and so my poor child was the means of saving Toronto where he had many partisans.'*

Shortly after the rebellion, the exploit of two of Captain de Grassi's daughters was recorded in the October 6th, 1838 issue of the New York *'Albion'*, which named Cornelia and Charlotte de Grassi as the girls who accompanied their father down the Don Valley to Toronto on the memorable night of December 4th, 1837. 'They left the de Grassi place in full moonlight traversing what is called bush or enclosed country. Between Helliwell's and Bennett's they fell in with the notorious Mathews and his party, forty-two in number. The presence of mind of Charlotte saved them.' The article conformed that Cornelia rode out to Montgomery's tavern and brought information to army headquarters to the effect that the numbers of the rebels had been greatly exaggerated.

Charlotte ran into an adventure of her own, when upon returning from Toronto she was fired upon and wounded by a large party of rebels near the corner of the bush before Sinclair's clearing (somewhere near Broadview Avenue and O'Connor Drive).

Cornelia followed the troops up Yonge Street and after the events of the day was on her way home to give her mother an accout of them. Arriving at the Don bridge, she discovered that Mathews had set it on fire. She returned to the city and gave the alarm.

The article in the *'Albion'* was reprinted in its entirety in a brochure entitled *'The Story of Charlotte and Cornelia de Grassi'*, prepared by Mr. Stewart Wallace, F.R.C.S.. Mr. Wallace also secured Captain de Grassi's diary which is now in the library of the University of Toronto.

In Mr. Wallace's opinion, Mackenzie's pamphlet *'Head's Flag of Truce'*,

published in 1853, tends to verify the exploit of Cornelia de Grassi. Mackenzie makes some mention of it in these words: *'Dr. Ralph then advised me not to go into the city till towards dark—he told us that Dr. Horne had employed a woman as a spy (de Grassi I think he called her), whom we let pass, and Dr.H. has persuaded Head to hold out, assuring him our numbers were less than we supposed.'*

In his brochure Mr. Wallace observes that the above quoted extract 'not only provides evidence from an unimpeachable source of the substantial accuracy of the story of Cornelia de Grassi, but it makes it clear that her exploit played an important part in the Rebellion of 1837 in Upper Canada. Up to Wednesday, December 6th, 1837, Sir Francis Bond Head had been in such a state of extreme 'funk' that he had placed his family on board a steamer in Toronto harbour but on receipt of the information brought to him by the thirteen year old Cornelia de Grassi, he decided to hold out. It is of course possible that Sir Francis Head may have received information in regard to the rebels from other sources as well, but it is clear that Wm.Lyon Mackenzie himself regarded Cornelia de Grassi's information as crucial.'

Mr. Wallace made a search of the Toronto papers in their references to the Mackenzie rebellion of 1837. He found nothing to confirm the story of the de Grassi girls' exploits.

Under date of July 4th, 1938, Mr. Mossom de Grassi Boyd of Bobcaygeon, Ontario, sent me a copy of Captain Phillips de Grassi's diary and which included mention of his daughter's adventure at Montgomery's tavern. It is the diary of an old man taking a long, perhaps last look down the corridor of his own past, and in which he desires to record truthfully and accurately the events of his life for the benefit and knowledge of those who follow him.

Mr. Bruce Lancaster, author of *'Bright to the Wanderer'* thought enough of the incident to include this conversation on page 275 of that book: 'Head knows everything about the people here. That nasty little de Grassi girl rode out there yesterday...It was Cornelia. She told her father and he told Colonel Fitzgibbon. Head knows that you haven't had much to eat. He knows how many men are here and how many have run away...'How could she know,' he stammered, 'She pushed him gently 'Get along to Mr. Mackenzie. Cornelia's seen her father's Company often enough. She said that you had about five hundred men here and that they were all hungry.'

I asked Mr. Lancaster what had led him to refer to the de Grassi girl in his book. In his letter to me of June 8th, 1948, he said: 'I have found nothing on the de Grassi family other than what I found in books such as those cited on the previous page...The rest of what I had consisted largely of writers saying that the story as I told it was pretty much as they had heard it in their childhood.'

Mr. Stewart Wallace quotes this further extract from the article in the *'Albion'*: 'After ridding herself of this party, she was again fired at from Watson's and was summoned to surrender, but at last reached the city bringing the news of the robbery of the public mail and describing the numbers of the rebels to be greatly exaggerated, many of them to be mere boys armed with club sticks, few possessing guns or rifles.'

Mr. Wallace points to several inaccuracies in the narrative of the *'Albion'*. For example, the rebels began to gather at Montgomery's farm on Yonge Streeet on December 4th and not on December 10th, 1837, for by that date they had been dispersed. And he adds: Captain de Grassi's property in the Don Valley was not 'a few miles from the city of Toronto, but was not much more than a mile from the city of 1837. There is to this day a de Grassi Street in the Riverdale section of Toronto which marks the neighbourhood of Captain de Grassi's property.'

I have since pointed out to Mr. Wallace that Captain de Grassi lived at the forks of the Don on parts of lots 6 and 7 Concession 3 and which I have known intimately since 1921. It is of some interest that I dug up in the old orchard of de Grassi's planting, a military buckle of the Napoleonic period and identified by the Royal Ontario Museum as such. Captain de Grassi's holdings were in the Don Valley. In his own words, he drew 200 acres of land on the Don in an area described as the Boatbildery. Old maps show the Boatbildery at the forks of the Don. My records are full of incidents relating to Phillipe de Grassi's presence in the Don Valley. I have spoken to persons who knew Phillipe de Grassi. De Grassi Street may have been named after one of his sons. It is several miles from the de Grassi homestead in the Don Valley.

Mr. Wallace concludes his brochure with the observation that:
'no one can pretend that two small girls of teen age, riding about on fiery ponies, during the Rebellion of 1837, altered the course of history, but no one can deny that they played a gallant and perhaps important part in the course of events during those far-off days.'

In January of 1954, I mentioned the facts of the de Grasso girls' exploits during a conference at which Florence Schill, a reporter of the *'Globe & Mail'* was present. On January 30th, 1954, a feature story headed *'Cornelia 13, Gallant Spy in 1837 Rebellion'* appeared in the *'Globe & Mail'*. As events transpired, it was picked up by The Canadian Press and made its way across Canada. This extract from the story is worthy of mention here.

'The Story first appeared in the New York *'Albion'* of October 6, 1838. The *'Albion'*, though a U.S. paper, had British leanings and regularly carried news of interest to Canadians. A yellowed clipping of the account sent by Colonel G.D.Collins, an officer of the U.S. army, and great-grandson of Phillipe de Grassi, to Mr. Wallace, started his research.'

'It was in 1941 that Mr. Stewart Wallace, librarian of the University of Toronto, presented his paper *'The Story of Charlotte and Cornelia de Grassi'* to the Royal Society of Canada.' The article also referred to myself as having obtained a copy of the personal reminiscences of Phillips de Grassi from Mossom de Grassi Boyd in 1938, in the course of collecting information on the family background of the pioneers of the Don Valley. 'It is interesting to note,' the article observes, 'that Mr. Wallace and Mr. Sauriol assembled the facts separately, Mr. Wallace working from the story in the 'Albion' to the family background, and Mr. Sauriol working from the family history to the story. Official reference to the deed of the de Grassi girls is confined to a listing in the Dictionary of Canadian Geography, under Phillipe de Grassi, which reads:

'In the Rebellion of 1837, two of his daughters, Cornelia (d. 1885) and Charlotte (d. 1872), played a romantic and adventurous part...'

I muse on this almost unknown episode of Canadian history when in a Summer evening I stroll about the acres which de Grassi pioneered (by the road which still bears the name of de Grassi hill) and gaze with affection at the ancient board dwelling, now freshly painted, which he inhabited and from which he set out with his two daughters on that memorable night of December 4th, 1837, to play his part in putting down the Mackenzie rebellion. A tree near the dwelling bears this sign: 'Historic site, de Grassi homestead 1832.'

Winter 1955

The Passing Scene

A Tribute to the things 'that used to be'

THERE USED TO BE on Donlands Ave. a giant oak tree where Billets Groceteria now stands, and alongside of it a coke path along which youths of the 20's used to ride their bicycles with dizzy speed. In the 20's John Hawthorne Taylor's mansion style house stood near the present corners of O'Connor Drive and Don Mills Road, across from it stood a pioneer dwelling, with lilacs growing in front of it. A man by the name of Murray kept bees there and sold honey to passers-by. At the top of Don Mills Road, where it descends into the Valley, stood another pioneer dwelling. A market garden stretched from Don Mills Road to Coxwell Ave., from the edge of the ravine to O'Connor Drive. Early in the Spring when the frost had left the ground, the first seeding of radishes took place. O'Connor Drive was a quaint little trail bordered with poplars—a favorite cycle ride to Woodbine Ave.

There used to be at the top of Woodbine Ave. a place called 'Bush-Inn', and beyond that the wilderness of one ravine after another until the east valley of the Don was reached. This used to be a great skiing country and hundreds of youths passed Saturday afternoons skiing and jumping along these ravines, now Parkview Hills subdivision.

This picturesque bridge over west Don River forks of the stream collapsed in the Summer of 1953. See The Cardinal Winter 1953 issue. It was used to connect Thorncliffe farm (in Leaside) with the farm buildings at the forks of the Don.

There used to be a bridge on Don Mills Road about where Todmorden Park adjoins it. Under this bridge ran the Canadian Northern line to Montreal. There used to be away back in the early days of the country, a boat bildery where Todmorden Park now lies, and on top of the hill across from the park on Don Mills Road there used to live a settler named Tumper, and the place used to be known as Tumper's mount. The north side of the mount was called greenlands, because of the heavy evergreen foliage which covered it and the snow used to lie there in places until July.

There used to be a saw mill in Taylor's bush. In 1914 a million and a half board feet of white pine were cut there. There used to be a carriage bridge over Taylor's creek. The road to which it led used to carry the traffic of its day to the Taylor farm, which used to be on the Parkview Hills subdivision. There used to be a wooden bridge supported with an iron frame over the Don by the forks of the stream, just about where the present arch bridge spans it, and there used to be several pop and refreshment stands where the Don Valley Art Club chalet now stands.

There used to be a dam on the west Don a little way up from the forks, a paper mill, and a number of barns and other buildings, where now scarcely a brick can be seen. There used to be a wooden bridge over the west Don leading to Thorncliffe. In the field across from the railway there used to be a large frame house. Old maps show that there was a small lake just up from the dam.

At the forks of the Don there used to be one of the finest farms in Ontario. An orchard stood on the slope where scarcely a tree remains. Deer used to roam enclosures on the farm.

There used to be runaway slaves from the U.S. in the valley and many of them used to work in the paper mills. There used to be a charcoal trade in the valley. The wood was burned for this purpose up valley where there used to be a logging road, the remains of which can still be seen. There used to be a saw mill on the Don just below de Grassi hill, and a fine swimming hole where the boys of several generations ago swam in the brook where they used to catch trout. There used to be salmon in the Don.

A man by the name of Skelhorne, a veteran of the Indian Mutiny, once lived in the de Grassi homestead. He used to bring scrap iron, bottles, etc. to the yard to sell it. There used to be a piggery on the place housing several hundred swine. There used to be a fellow who made his living cutting wood and used a model T Ford to run up and down the ice on the Don in winter to bring it in. Herds of cattle used to roam the valley by the forks, and at that time there never used to be any weeds in the valley.

Spring 1956

How It All Started

IN SUPPORT OF MY INTEREST in the Don Valley, it can be said that I have lived the life; as a boy tramping its wooded reaches, as a youth pitting his energy against five acres of rundown land and a dilapidated farm dwelling; as a man fighting a long hard fight for its preservation.

I first set foot on my acres at the Forks of the Don in January of 1927. From that date on, I thought only to turn them into a place of beauty. Forest trees were planted by the thousands, and an orchard too, which grew to fruitfulness. Rich soil was wrested from sod and twitch grass, and became a garden land in which fine fruits and vegetables grew.

I did just about everything on my place. I gathered the notes which made up my manuscript of the Don Valley. I made maple syrup from trees of my own planting. I canned fruit and vegetables, built a root house, kept a goat, a few pigs, chickens. I made a wild flower garden, established a bird sanctuary, built bridges which floods invariably washed out, dug wells, kept bees, made a log cabin retreat where most of The Cardinal was written. I produced several manuscripts, *'Fourteen Years on Four Acres'*. *'Ashes and Embers'* (the adventures of a boy in the Don Valley), *'One Man's Harvest'*. Perhaps it can be said that conservation on the Don stemmed largely from my pioneer conception of the Don Valley's importance as an area to be preserved, a one-man battle that I carried on for many years. The record of those years will support the statement.

As for the dwelling, it became a bower of tranquillity and repose; over the years its physical appearance was entirely changed. The touch of a woman's hand made the place fit to live in.

How I bought my acres is a story in itself and a strengthening of my belief that dreams do come true. Perhaps I bought them because at that time no one had given the Forks of the Don any attention. It was hill-billy country, back-wash of a pioneer day and of no importance.

It so happened that my cottage was erected in 1899 as a dwelling for a man who worked on the John Hawthorne Taylor farm, just up the pine-clad slope above it, now Parkview Hills. The land had been pioneered by de Grassi, as his Government grant of 1833. Then it went to the Taylors, and from John H.Taylor to the Canadian Northern Railway, when the Company laid a line through the Valley in 1907. The stream which now flows past my place made a wide curve to the north in its original course. The railway changed that, and the severed fragment of the river became the frog pond where de Grassi had a mill dam.

The place went from bad to worse. Successive tenancies at rentals of $5.00 a month left in their wake nails as hooks, doors without locks, a crumbling chimney, porous shingles, cheap wall paper, brown woodwork, and outside walls that had never been painted. As the cottage and grounds stand today there is probably not a prettier spot in the Greater Toronto area. It reflects in a hundred ways the enthusiastic planning of the years.

In 1927, my acres were bare, save for two old apple trees of de Grassi's planting, an ancient willow tree still standing today and the dwelling. No water, no light, no convenience whatsoever. There are many books on the market of the 'We took to the country' type. I feel reasonably sure that I have lived my own life of the outdoors of a calibre which would make many of the 'back to nature' authors envious—and this on the threshold of a great growing city. Of the thousands of persons who motor along Don Mills Road, few realize what lies behind the sign of the wooden Cardinal which can be seen on the peak of my cottage.

I never gave it a name, although I often tried. *'The Lily of the Valley'* and many other possible descriptions went their way as somewhat poor pictures of the portrait I carried within me, so the place became simply known as the cottage: 'Le Chalet' as we say in French. When I used either term it meant everything. It evoked my pioneer days on the place, the cavalcade of events which marched through the years of my occupancy; the memories of a friendly wood stove in winter, of the spiral sparks of flaming hemlock, of the outdoor fireplace, of the friendly faces so often seen about a living room

The dwelling in July of 1935. Later a room was built under its peak and a dormer window appeared over the roof.

whose story was one of really being lived in.

And so the cottage stands today, fifty-six years old; companion, one might say, of a lifetime, and for still another lifetime. But, as we so well know, there is nothing surer in life than change. I was standing in a pine grove of my own planting one day last June, when two men came along with maps in their hands. They were trying to locate the position of a roadway in relation to my acres. To any but my unbelieving eyes, the plan was clear enough; the road led across the meadows through my orchard, to the plateau on which stood the cottage. That road as planned would wipe out the work of thirty years. I tried to be reasonable about it, arguing that after all, nothing could go on unaltered forever; the place had served its main purpose in my life. Somewhere other potential beauty spots were waiting for the attention I could bestow upon them.

The route of the Don Valley parkway was made public on November 30th, 1955. I saw the maps during a preview showing of that date. Here again it was a sad blow; the maps confirmed what I had previously suspected. It seemed that my acres and cottage were destined to disappear under a sheet of macadam.

It has been said that happiness is pleasure without regret, that a world lies in the stream which flows through one's orchard, if one has the imagination to fully exploit one's surroundings. I have been somewhat as

138

The cedar log cabin, where most of 'The Cardinal' was written. It was a few feet away from the cottage kitchen at the entrance of the wild flower garden. The path to the right led to the bee hives. (Photo Feb. 1, 1954.)

The de Grassi homestead as it appeared in December 1954. Note the sign on the tree surmounted with a painting of a Cardinal. It reads: 'Conservation Centre, Don Valley Conservation Association'. This photo will offer an interesting comparison with later photos showing the gradual development of the de Grassi homestead as a conservation centre.

Thoreau who *'travelled far in Concord.'* I have no regrets; and I have travelled intensely in the valley which lay at my door. I have lived of the simple, satisfying things of life in the abundance of successive seasons and their magnificent bounty.

Mine was a philosophy of the fullness of little things, of the need for the feel of the earth, of the companionship of nature. In the realm of the outdoors with its sunsets, woodlands, birds, flowers, fruits of the soil and fruits of the mind. I found all that a nature-loving man could wish for. I knew the fragrance of the Balm of gilead after a June rain; the restfulness of water splashing over stones; of the peeping of the first hylas of spring. It was a simple life, completely divorced from the things I did for a living. That is why I loved it. It got me away from business. It was a sure refuge from problems renewed daily. 'Old Murph', the bee man, started me on bee keeping because he said it would take my mind off my work—and it did.

What the place meant to me and the good it did me is best appraised through 28 years of diaries which record my impressions from day to day all during that time. Whenever I had a problem to solve or tried to sum-up some situation, or myself, I wrote it down. Soon, I was writing about everything. I wrote by the fireside, or seated on a log deep in the woods, or beside the tiny paddle wheel mill I had set up in the stream. I wrote about the chores of the garden, of the tinkle of the sap in the pails I hung onto the maple trees in April. I never travelled without pencil and paper and not infrequently got out of bed in the middle of the night to set some thought to imagery in a prose I wished to retain. I never looked on my place as merely a physical thing. To me it lived. It was a part of me as I had become part of it. A friend once said it was my brain child.

One by one I have seen the landmarks of my day and of my surroundings disappear and the old-timers as well. The farmlands, the trails, the trees, buried in, covered over or chopped down. The stream is not as clear as it used to be. The sylvan aspect of a woodland realm of 28 years ago has been altered, and will change still more.

Yet much of the valley still remains, is still beautiful, is still worth saving.

And in conclusion, a word of appreciation for the companions who over the years beat a path to my door. And a kindly thought too for those men and women who gave unstintingly of their time to save what could be salvaged of the valley for a future generation.

As for my holdings, their fate is in the road planners' hands. They may disappear or they may not. If they do not it is likely that there will be at the Forks of the Don a nature sanctuary of no small importance. If they should be sacrificed, then one more landmark will disappear and with it the bountiful source of 'One Man's Harvest'.

Don Valley History

The Mississauga Indians

encamped along the Don. They were so named by the French. The remains of Indian encampments have been frequently found along the banks of the Don and in the flats in the neighbourhood of Riverdale Park. Withrow Avenue east of the Don, was the site of an Indian village. Indian relics have been picked up in the Valley, including a stone plow, a tomahawk blade, a flint skinning knife, an egg-shaped stone used to pound corn in a wooden vessel.

Naming the Don

On August 11, 1793, Mrs. Simcoe wrote: *'this evening we went to see a creek which is to be called the river Don.'* The Indian name for the Don river was WONSCOTEONOCH, signifying black burnt lands of the Don watershed previously swept by fire. The first English maps designate the Don by the Indian name, NECHENG QUA KEKONK. The surveyor, Alexander Aitkin, used this name in September, 1788, referring to the Don in his survey of the land purchased at Toronto from the Indians.

Toronto Marsh, Ashbridge's Bay and the Peninsula

The Toronto Marsh and Ashbridge's Bay in their original state were one of the leading bird sanctuaries of the continent, as these references imply: *'The River Don empties itself into the harbour a little above town running through a marsh.' 'A mere swamp, a tabgled wilderness, the birch, hemlock, tamarack, growing down to the water's edge, even into the lake.' 'Southward was a great stretch of marsh with the blue lake along the horizon.' 'Many of the rare bird records of Ontario were from Toronto marsh. This wonderful bird paradise is a thing of the past.'*

As for Ashbridge's Bay, only a tiny fragment of the original bay and adjacent marsh now remains. The Ashbridge's Bay Reclamation scheme got under way in 1890-92.

Old maps of Toronto show a long narrow peninsula bordered on one side by the lake and on the other by the marsh. It jutted westward from the foot of Woodbine Ave. to Gibraltar Point. The halfway mark of the peninsula was in line with the mouth of the Don. The peninsula was considered healthy by the Indians. It was at one time stocked with goats. Catfish Jo's island lay at the mouth of the Don river. The eastern gap of Toronto Bay was broken through by a storm in 1871 or 1872.

Gooderham and Worts Windmill

stood at the mouth of the Don at the foot of the present-day Cherry Street. The mill was erected in 1831-32. At that time a military block house stood a short distance east of the mill.

Early Aspect of Don River

'In the spring and summer, a pull up the Don when its banks were in a primeval state was something to be enjoyed. After passing certain potasheries and distilleries the meadow land began to widen out.' In Dr. Scadding's day, the Don was the main artery of winter travel. 'Down the river, every day came a cavalcade of strong sleighs heavily laden with cordwood, sawn lumber, hay.' About 1870 hops were grown in the Don flats for use in local breweries.

In their orginal state, the banks and slopes of the Don valley from Queen Street to Riverdale Park were much higher than at present. The slopes were graded and the soil from them used for 'fill' to level up the adjoining marsh.

Riverdale Park

In 1856 Toronto purchased 119 acres of land from the Scadding estate. In 1890 the city set aside all lands acquired from the Scadding estate for park purposes, excepting the jail property. The present Riverdale Park covers 162 acres. The Riverdale Zoo was established in 1899. The Riverdale flats were once the jail farm. In the early days of Riverdale Park, red-coated militia regiments fought each other in sham battles which took place in that part of the Don Valley.

John Coon

One of the first settlers on the Don. A sergeant in Butler's Rangers. On Sept. 11, 1793, Mrs. Simcoe wrote: *'rowed six miles up the Don to Coon's who has a farm under a hill covered with pines.' 'I land to see the shingles made,'* she said. Coon's farm lay in the Don Valley between Rosedale ravine and the present pit of the Don Valley brick works.

John Elmsley

Appointed in 1796 Chief Justice for Upper Canada. He drew as a grant lot 14, concession 2, on the Don. He was a close friend of D.W.Smith, the surveyor-general.

The Lower Don as a Navigable Stream

In 1889 the Don was part of a grandiose plan to bring vessels up the Don to Gerrard Street. Wharf accommodation was proposed along the banks to link up with the Don Improvement. Swing bridges were to provide an unobstructed passage for all shipping.

While all plans relating to larger vessels never matured, there was considerable shipping of a lesser kind on the Don to Winchester Street. Schooners unloaded at factory wharves in the vicinity of Gerrard Street. The 'Minnie Kidd', a ferry, went up the Don to Winchester Street. It is said that the steam barge 'Gordon Jerry' delivered plate glass along the Don. Smaller steam barges, 'May Bird' and 'Honey Dew' had telescoping masts and hinged funnels and delivered general freight to the Gerrard Street landing. They also unloaded fertilizer for fruit farms at Jordan. Coghill's dry-dock lay at the mouth of the Don. The schooner 'Eric Belle' was laid up at the mouth of the Don in 1894. Steps led from the docks at Gerrard Street to the banks above.

The Brooks Bush Gang

'To venture above Winchester Street,' said an old-timer, 'was to enter territory where gambling, cock-fighting, and bull pitting flourished.' The Brooks bush gang flourished (about 1862) on a forty acre heavily-wooded area, just east of the Don river. It consisted of a score of hoodlums who terrorized the surrounding neighborhood. Ernest Thompson Seton said that members of the Brooks gang destroyed his cabin in the Fall of 1875. (See 'Two Little Savages').

Geology of the Don Valley Clay Pit

The Don Valley brickyard pit has been visited and admired by geologists from all over the world. It has become famous among students of the Pleistocene, that is to say the epoch of the last glaciation. The pit has been described as the most interesting section on the continent. It has given collectors the widest range of fossils in the country, and has disclosed the relations of one bed to another. Accordingly the history of the last glaciation could be worked out with some certainty. Shells, nuts, pieces of wood have been found at a depth of 50 feet below the floor of the Don Valley, An extinct species of Pleistocene maple has been found buried along the Don. In 1915 excavations for the pier of the Bloor Street viaduct showed stratified silt and sand containing logs of wood for 32 feet below the level of the river, and at this depth just above the shale, the skull of a bear was found.

Broadview Ave. or the Mill Road

On March 1, 1798, an order was given to Timothy Skinner Sr. to open up a road from the Kingston Road east of the Don bridge between lots 14 and 15 northwards to the Don Mills. This was the original Don Mills Road, later Broadview Ave. It has been decribed by Wm.Lea as 'a mere wagon track winding among trees and underbrush. It curved round the bank of the Don to the top of the hill and down to the mills.' The original entrance to the mills (which stood across the road from Fantasy Farm of today) was near Don Valley Drive, and not Pottery Road which is the present-day entrance to the valley.

'About a half-mile north of the Don Mills on lot 15 concession 2 there was a saw mill built by David Secord about 1815.' This mill was either on the site of, or close to the site of the Taylor *'middle mill'* at the foot of Beechwood Drive in East York.

Wm.Lea

was the son of John Lea who came to York about 1820. William was born in Lancashire in 1814. He wrote extensively on the Don. His address on the Don to the Canadian Institute was published in the *Toronto Evening Telegram* of Jan. 17th, 1881, and February 4th, 1881. We owe to Wm.Lea an authentic account of life on the Don in the early 19th century. Wm.Lea is the forgotten historian. He wrote with feeling. For example: 'This wooded portion of the river was one of the most beautiful walks that could be taken. Here was quiet, only the rippling of the water over a stoney bed, or the whirr of wild ducks, or the partridge drumming in the distance. The water was pebbly and clear, the banks covered with evergreens and trees, forming a canopy of beautiful green. A temple not made with hands.' That was the lower Don Valley as he knew it.

Boat Building on the Don

D.W.Smith the surveyor general of Simcoe's time, owned the west half of lots 6 and 7, concession 3, East York, on the present site of Todmorden Park. A map in the D.W.Smith papers shows a *'mill seat'* on lot 6. D.W.Smith is described on Map A32 (Dept, of Lands, Forests, Toronto) as a boat builder. Map A33 inscribes lot 6 and 7 with the name D.W.Smith, then the initials T.G.S. and the notation *'boat builder'*. Phillipe de Grassi writing in 1833 said: *'I drew as my grant parts of lots 6 and 7 two hundred acres on the Don, on what was then known as the boat bildery.'* Nowhere in Don valley history have I seen conclusive proof that a boat bildery existed on the Don, yet it seems that such an industry was at one time in operation.

The last Saw mill in Don Valley stood north of present Bloor Street viaduct. This mill supplied building wood for the neighbourhood. It was operated by The Don Kindling Company. Photo: circa 1900.

Lewis Vail

was one of the earliest Don Valley pioneers. He applied for Government land in 1794. He was granted lot 4 concession 3. His farm entered the east Don Valley about where Woodbine Ave. would cross it, if extended. Remnants of his orchard are seen in this area. The ruins of the foundation of his dwelling are still discernible and the lilac bushes which he planted have spread to cover an entire slope of the Don Valley.

The Latham Mill

Remains of the mill race are visible by the clay banks swimming hole. Isaac Latham operated a mill here in the 50's.

The Martin Brothers

Two old men, John and Art Martin, lived at the edge of the Macleans sugar bush about fifty feet from the east Don river. Up until 1920, the dwelling was still in evidence, also the remnants of a garden. A person who knew them writes: *'We missed them sadly when the Martin clan decided they were too old to go on living there. They were never really happy after they left the valley, and both died soon after, probably much sooner than if left in their beloved valley.'* (C.S. Note: they died in an old man's home.)

The Don School

stood on the north-east corner of Don Mills Road and Lawrence Ave. east. It was built in 1883 at a cost of 84 pounds. It was one storey high, and was made of red brick. It measured forty by twenty feet. It was demolished in April 1948. The first Don school (a log cabin) was built in 1837 on the south-east corner of Wm.Gray's farm, lot 9, Con. 3.

The Hogg Family

John Hogg located on lot 7, con. 3 in 1835. His farm was across the east Don from the present disposal plant of the Don Mills development. Descendants of the family lived on the homestead until 1947. Unti 1950, remains of a mill dam could be seen in the east Don, near the disposal plant.

William and Alexander Gray

The Grays were neighbours of the Hoggs. They settled on the east Don, lot 8, con. 3. William erected a grist mill, Alexander a saw mill. Both mills were located below the pond on *'Donalda'* farm, now part of Don Mills Development. Mr. Wm.Gray's last mill was standing in 1950, encased within the more modern framework of a Donalda farm barn.

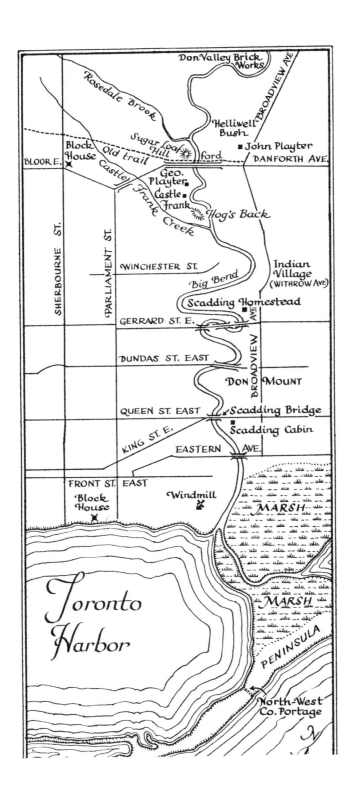

Charles Sauriol

Charles Sauriol was born a stone's throw from the lower Don River near Queen Street. His father came to Toronto to dredge the Don. Young Charles always had an inherent love of the Don Valley. His hero of the Valley was Ernest Thompson Seton, whose books *'Two Little Savages'* and *'Wild Animals I Have Known'* were largely related to Seton's Don Valley experiences.

By 1920, Sauriol had joined the 45th East Toronto Troop of Boy Scouts, and this association increased his awareness and experiences with the Valley. Already at that time Charles was interested in stopping by to talk to descendents of original pioneer families, collecting photos and stories as he went.

In 1927 Charles acquired, at the forks of the Don River, a run-down frame dwelling, and four acres of land. The property was known as 'The Lily of the Valley'. By 1930 he started writing a history of the Valley in manuscript form that required more than twenty years to complete.

In 1950 he co-founded the Don Valley Conservation Association to protest emerging threats to Sauriol's notion of an unspoiled woodland kingdom at Toronto's doorstep. 'The Cardinal' was written and published at this time.

Ironically, after having done so much to save the valley, his holdings were expropriated for the Don Valley Parkway. The cottage was torn down. Sauriol then moved to the historic de Grassi Homestead across the river and here he re-built all of his values. Ten years later he was again expropriated and for a second time, lost all of his Don Valley possessions.

In 1957 Charles Sauriol was appointed to The Metropolitan Toronto and Region Conservation Authority and served for fourteen consecutive years as a member of the Executive Committee and Chairman of the Conservation Areas Advisory Board. In this role he made incalculable contributions to the preservation of the Don Valley.

In 1968 he joined the Nature Conservancy of Canada as Co-Administrator and Projects Director.

At 'Press Time', Charles Sauriol, was appointed to the position of Executive Director of the Nature Conservancy of Canada.

Design by John Elphick

Typesetting by Erin Graphics

Lithography by Maracle Press

COVER

Clay banks swimming hole. 1939.

Don Valley Parkway Courtesy of York University Archives